/MIKE FENTON

BRITISH BUSES
AROUND THE
WORLD

PSL **Patrick Stephens, Cambridge**

First published 1982

British Library Cataloguing in Publication Data

Fenton, Mike
   British buses around the world.
   1. Motor buses — Pictorial works
   I. Title
   629.2'2233'0222   TL232

   ISBN 0-85059-594-0

Set in 9 on 10 pt Univers by Manuset Limited, Baldock,
Herts. Printed and bound in Great Britain on 100 gsm
Fineblade coated cartridge by The Garden City Press,
Letchworth, Herts, for the publishers Patrick Stephens
Limited, Bar Hill, Cambridge, CB3 8EL, England.

CONTENTS

INTRODUCTION

For many years I have thought that there should be a book about buses in operation overseas but specifically those with a British connection, ie, with British-made chassis or bodywork, either exported new or at second hand. It is surprising that the subject has been neglected for such a long time as a huge number of interesting, unusual or downright unbelievable buses have seen service in the world, a suitable selection being found within the pages of this volume.

Sadly British-made buses are no longer as common a sight in the world as they were, say, 30 years ago. Indeed the present situation is nowhere near as good as it should be from a sales point of view. It is not the job of the author to delve too deeply into the reasons for this decline but, clearly, some companies lived for too long on past glories when they did have the best product, and became complacent in the face of competition from European and Japanese manufacturers for their traditional markets. There are, of course, still many well satisfied and enthusiastic purchasers of British-made PSVs overseas but the author has heard the complaint 'they would not supply what we wanted when it was wanted' far too often for comfort. Once a market is lost it becomes difficult indeed to recapture.

On a happier note, the author has some very pleasant memories of overseas travel and friendships made with enthusiasts in foreign countries. Yes, there are enthusiasts overseas and not just in the Commonwealth countries, for the breed is also known to exist in Finland, Sweden, Belgium, Spain, Holland and Malta! Should this book prove to be successful then it is possible that a second volume would follow and, for this reason, the author would be very pleased to hear from any reader having photographs of suitable overseas material with a special emphasis on South America, the Far East, Africa and some European countries including Cyprus, Greece and the Canary Islands.

Mike Fenton

ACKNOWLEDGEMENTS

Of the photographs used in this book, about one third were taken by myself, the rest having been borrowed from more than 20 other photographers. My sincere thanks are extended to all of them for allowing me to use their work herein. Indeed, were it not for the efforts of a select band of intrepid explorers of the 1950s and '60s many fascinating vehicles would never have been recorded at all.

In particular I would like to single out a handful of individuals for special thanks. Bruce Tilley of Melbourne, a good friend of many years, took the Australasian photographs, plus a few from other countries, as well as supplying 'gen' and checking some text. Ron Phillips of Warrington deserves many thanks for the supplying of information and photographs as does another good friend, Ian Charlton from Sunderland, a 'bashing' companion of many years. Frank Lestrade of Haarlem, Holland, has provided a wealth of information on Dutch vehicles as well as sending me photographs produced by the Dutch Bus Preservation Society, the SVA.

Special thanks are offered to overseas coachbuilders and the hundreds of overseas operators visited, much to their astonishment, over the years. Although we usually arrived unheralded, the hand of friendship has almost always been offered. What is more, in addition to cups of coffee and meals being offered, fleet details were retrieved from obscure corners or elderly vehicles fished out of the depths of garages for the purpose of photography, sometimes leaving behind fume-filled scenes of chaos!

Some of the data used in this volume has been collected on the author's own travels with the balance being supplied by friends or the PSV Circle, an organisation which anyone with an interest in buses is recommended to join. Details of membership may be obtained by writing to; Mr A.G. Johnson FCA, 52 Old Park Ridings, Grange Park, London N21 2ES.

CAPITAL EXPORTS

Exacting standards of construction and maintenance have greatly contributed to the sales appeal of former London buses. Indeed, so widespread have sales of London buses been that it is probably true to say that in their time they have been just as familiar to the inhabitants of Colombo and Corunna as they have to the residents of Chelsea and Chiswick.

During 1946, in order to alleviate a shortage of double-deckers, London Transport purchased a batch of some 65 Leyland-bodied Leyland PD1s. These buses of the manufacturer's standard design were, of course, non-standard in the capital and so had a short life in London, being withdrawn during 1954 and 1955, most if not all going to operators in Yugoslavia. Some went to Sarajevo and Mostar, but H5999, formerly STD 140 (HLW 69) was based at Split on the Adriatic coast. In this view taken in 1959 it is about to leave Trogir on the 30 km journey to its home town. Although this vehicle ran in virtually original condition, several buses of this type were rebuilt with entrances on the Yugoslavian nearside. By the mid-1960s few remained in service *(D.W.K. Jones)*.

Right Two or three years prior to the sale of STDs a batch of T class AEC Regal 0662s was exported to Yugoslavia. Auto Transportno Poduzece of Sibenik were the owners of H6152, a Chiswick-bodied vehicle of 1938, ex-T 490, ELP 214. Like the STD class, many of these buses were used by their new owners in original condition with, from a Yugoslavian point of view, the entrance on the wrong side. In practice this unusual arrangement posed few problems owing mainly to the scarcity of other road traffic at that time *(D. W. K. Jones).*

Right T 543 was another vehicle exported to Yugoslavia where it became Split Transport 30. Remarkably, although the Chiswick body had been rebuilt with a new entrance, the bus still sported not only its Central Area red livery but also its British registration number! The driver of ELP 267 proudly poses in front of his charge in Trogir during 1954 *(D. W. K. Jones).*

Below right By the time this AEC Renown was photographed in 1955 in Nish, it had two arduous years of operation in Yugoslavia to its credit in addition to its 22 years of service in London! Not surprisingly, the former LT 1098, GO 7144, was by this time looking rather down at heel. As may be seen, the original front entrance had been panelled over, passengers entering via the rear emergency door and leaving via a new exit cut into the English offside at the front, a conversion guaranteed further to weaken an already geriatric LGOC body. In addition to the illustrated C5563 at least one further example of the class operated at Nish at the same time—LT 1028 which carried the Yugoslavian registration C5566 *(J. C. Gillham).*

Left STLs could be found in quantity in Skopje, most, like M2701, operating in almost original condition, the only concession to driving on the right being the repositioning of the entrance at the *back* of the body. This new entrance was situated at the foot of the stairs and had a sliding door, being somewhat akin to the emergency exits found on United Kingdom double-deckers having platform doors. At least one STL, M2901, was cut down to single-deck, although whether this was deliberate policy or simply the result of an accident or structural problems is unclear *(J.C. Gillham)*.

Left The former identity of C4863 photographed in Smederevo, Yugoslavia, in 1955 is not known, although it is quite clearly a Birmingham RC&W-bodied AEC Q of the 4Q4 class delivered during 1935-6 and withdrawn during the period 1952-4 *(J.C. Gillham)*.

Below left The records of Frank Aquilina, one of Malta's coachbuilders, detail that in August 1957 the body of a second-hand AEC was completed for an operator on Gozo. What the records do not state is that this bus, No 1948, was almost certainly an ex-London Transport Q type, nor is this the only such example in Malta. Private hire bus No 20 of Zarb, Gzira, which also has Aquilina bodywork, is thought to be a similar Q type. It should be noted that engines in both these vehicles were repositioned in a more usual location at the front of the chassis. Unfortunately it has not as yet proved possible to identify exactly which chassis were involved, partly because little official documentation exists in Malta relating to PSVs and partly because chassis number plates, etc, tend to be hidden under bodywork or removed altogether. In addition to this pair, one further Q type operated in Malta and this has been identified as Q103, CGJ 208. It entered Maltese service in 1953, as Malta 1860, on the Birkirkara route still in original condition with Birmingham RC&W bodywork. Somewhat incongruously, towards the end of its life it sported a Bedford SB type grille fitted, it must be stressed, at the front and not on the offside as may have been feared! By late 1969 it was derelict in the M'sida valley although, at the time of writing, 1948 and 20 continue in service *(M. Fenton)*.

Right A large proportion of the 1935 batch of Country Area Leyland Cub KP03 buses was exported, many being sold for further service in Ceylon, or Sri Lanka as it is now known, and Belgium. One of these attractive little buses, the former C29, BXD 654 was photographed in Ostend in 1951 whilst working for a company from nearby Stene, its Short Bros body having been suitably rebuilt with a front entrance on the driver's side. In Belgium it carried the registration 117579 (W.J. Wyse).

Right In 1951 this Gardner 5LW-engined Guy Arab I was plodding around the streets of Barking as London Transport G 64, GLL 564. A couple or so years later, in chassis form, it had migrated to the sun and the fleet Asociación Patronal de Jardineras Guagas of Gran Canaria. After receiving new locally-constructed single-deck bodywork it became APJG 67, GC-8935, re-joining in this fleet some of its former stablemates similarly rebodied. In keeping with the vast majority of Arab Is, double-deck bodywork built to Ministry of Supply wartime utility standards was originally fitted, in this case by Park Royal (M. Dryhurst).

Right Transportes Guanarteme of Las Palmas, Gran Canaria, operated two Weymann-bodied AEC Regals of the elegant 9T9 class, both dating from 1936. Interestingly this pair worked for more years in the Canary Islands than in London, being acquired about 1954 and lasting until the early 1970s. GC-8340, illustrated, was T 415, CLX 563, in Green Line service, its sister GC-8432 being T 423 CLX 371. Both were rebuilt as B34D but additionally by 1961, GC-8340 had received a rather bulbous home-made radiator surround utilising a Commer Commando type grille which did nothing to improve its appearance (M. Dryhurst).

Left Coruña in north-western Spain at one time boasted two operators of London trolleybuses. An inter-urban company, Compania de Trolebuses Coruña–Carballo operated, as may be deduced from the title, to Carballo some 33 km distant using seven Q1s, but the main Q1 operator was Tranvías de la Coruña who ultimately acquired a fleet of 29, some arriving via other Spanish systems. Most remained as double-deckers, rebuilt as H36/19D, but a few were cut down to single-deck including TC No 50 which was formerly LT 1784, HYM 784 (*D.A. Jones*).

Left The Spanish plaza (enclave) of Melilla on the Mediterranean coast of northern Morocco had three London buses in operation during the late 1950s. One, ML-4599, was an ex-Central Area AEC Q/Park Royal of the 5Q5 class (Q106-185 series). The others were ML-3953 and ML-3994, being former Green Line underfloor-engined Leyland FECs from the series TF 14-88; they were new in 1939. A further Melilla-registered TF was ML-3996, although it was working in Algeciras in southern Spain when photographed in 1959. In all cases the Chiswick-built bodies were subjected to a number of alterations including the provision of rear entrances and front exits on the right-hand side and, more obviously, rebuilding with full fronts in an attempt to improve air flow to their radiators. The other Spanish enclave of Ceuta, some 250 km to the west of Melilla, also had TFs. At least two are known to have operated here; CE-2428 and CE-3531. Unlike the Melilla-registered examples, this pair soldiered on in half cab condition (*A.R. Phillips*).

Left The first double-deck buses to run in Kenya were two ex-London Transport G class Guy Arab IIs acquired in 1952 by Kenya Bus Services Ltd. These pioneers which had joined a fleet already containing a sizeable representation of Guys of Marks II and III, were soon followed, in 1953, by three further examples from the same source. 1953 was also the year in which the associated company, Kenya Bus Services (Mombasa) Ltd, purchased their first double-deckers for operation in that city. One of these D 55, KAC 771, is shown in operation during the time of the Mau-Mau emergency, probably during 1956. It was new in 1945 as London Transport G 386, HGC 165, and apart from an increase in the number of opening windows, its utility Weymann bodywork remained largely unaltered (*R.F. Mack*).

Right Apart from being sold for normal stage service overseas RTs and RTLs have also been in demand with foreign buyers conscious of the novelty value of double-deckers for special tours, etc, in countries unfortunate enough to be without this British institution. Such operation is, however, not without its problems; low bridges, overhead wires and height regulations all providing headaches for the would-be operator. Swiss height regulations necessitated the rebuilding of RT 2156, KGK 965. Careful study will reveal that its Weymann body has been reduced in height by the removal of a little over 1 ft of panelling from the upper deck. Rather than have an impossibly low headroom in the upper deck, the floor was also lowered marginally thus averaging out the loss of inches between both decks. This amazing vehicle, found by chance near Lausanne in 1980, gives a fascinating insight into what a lowbridge RT might have looked like had it ever been produced *(M. Fenton).*

Right 25 ex-London Transport Q1 trolleybuses were purchased by Transportes Urbanos del Gran Bilbao SA, a municipal operator in the Basque region of northern Spain, 23 of which entered service between 1961 and 1968. These were the odd numbered vehicles of the batch 1843-1891, but excluding 1877 and 1887. In Bilbao their Metro-Cammell bodies were converted to H43/8D layout, the lower deck having much standing space in lieu of seating, although the conductor was seated. It may be thought merely coincidental that TUGB 875, illustrated, was formerly London Transport 1875, but in fact all 23 of this type simply ran with their London numbers reduced by 1,000 thus rendering identification easy for any interested party *(J. G. S. Smith).*

Right Two Q1s purchased by TUGB entered service, but not as trolleybuses, for the former London Transport 1877 and 1887 were lengthened by approximately 5 ft and fitted with underfloor Leyland diesel engines and pre-selective gearboxes! Unlike TUGB's trolleybuses which retained their original driving positions, the two motor-bus rebuilds were converted to left-hand drive, an alteration necessitated by the new front door position *(G. Elliott).*

Left In the interests of standardisation the newly created Ceylon Transport Board purchased several hundred London Transport buses, starting in the late 1950s and continuing throughout the '60s. Double-deckers bought by the CTB included RT, RTL and RTW types, 23sri1350 being, believe it or not, an RT! After several years of operation in conventional double-deck form the former RT 787, JXC 150, received new single-deck bodywork by its owner, who had by this time been retitled as the Sri Lanka Central Transport Board. When photographed in April 1981 it was one of only three RTs still in CTB passenger service although a few others, similarly rebuilt, were seeing further service with private operators in Colombo *(B. S. Harris)*.

Left Former London buses first appeared on the streets of Sarajevo, Yugoslavia, in 1952 with the acquisition of several G class Guy Arabs. By the mid-1960s the Gs were gone but the purchase of 40 RTLs compensated for the loss. Usually they were employed on tramway feeder services like the former RTL 1110, LYF 34, seen here some 12 km from the city centre at Ilidza, the outer terminus of Sarajevo's main tram route. As may be seen from the illustration the Park Royal body of GSP No 42, SA-54-16 had, like its sisters, been rebuilt with its entrance on the right, the stairs being repositioned in the opposite rear corner of the body ascending in a clockwise direction *(J. G. S. Smith)*.

Below left Of course, some 'London Transport' double-deckers never ran within 200 miles of the capital. A little known part of Hammersmith perhaps with an 11 awaiting departure for Liverpool Street? Not quite, although Victoria displayed on the blind is certainly served by RM4, the State of Victoria, for this is a vehicle used on charter work by London Transport Tours Pty Ltd of Aspendale, Victoria, Australia. The vehicle, which is obviously a Bristol Lodekka/Eastern Coachworks, was chosen because height regulations in Victoria prohibited the operation of full height double-deckers. Originally LHO-888 had been Crosville Motor Services DLG879, 836 AFM, an LD6G model of 1956. On arrival in Australia in October 1972 it was repainted red, given London Transport fleetnames and the number RM4, this number being chosen in recognition of the solitary ECW-bodied Routemaster, although that particular vehicle was first numbered CRL4 and later RMC4 and always in green livery *(B. A. Tilley)*.

NEEDLES IN A HAYSTACK

British-made buses in France and Switzerland are so rare that the task of finding them may be compared with searching for a needle in a haystack.

The Geneva operator, Dubois, owned this 1956 Gangloff-bodied AEC Reliance until the early 1970s. It will be noted that this operator specified a right-hand drive chassis, although this was by no means unusual in Swiss buses of the period. It was thought that with this layout drivers could more accurately position their vehicles relative to the edges of Alpine roads than was possible with left-hand drive. The chassis of GE·96370 was of the MU3RAE heavy-duty export type, chassis number MU3RAE352 *(B.A. Tilley)*.

Left The robust Leyland Royal Tiger Worldmaster was purchased by at least two Swiss companies. In 1963 Auto AG Schwyz took delivery of five LCRT1/1 models with bodies constructed in Italy by Orlandi. These vehicles had seating for 29 passengers and standing room for a further 51, plus outside racks at the rear for skis. SZ·10117 is shown in this 1980 photograph still wearing pale green and primrose livery, a colour scheme in the process of being replaced by Switzerland's all pervading orange livery *(M. Fenton)*.

Left Schwyz's final Worldmasters, delivered in 1973, were fitted with Swiss-built Ramseier bodies although, like the earlier Orlandi-bodies batch, three-door bodywork was specified for SZ·5004 and its companion SZ·5006 *(M. Fenton)*.

Left In 1980 Leylands were to be found in the town of Schaffhausen close to the German border in the northern part of Switzerland with A. Rattin & Co. Six were owned; all were Worldmasters and, apart from one exception, all Hess-bodied standee vehicles, SH·210 being an LERT2A/1 model placed in service during 1972. Seats are provided for 30 persons with space for a further 56 standing passengers *(M. Fenton)*.

Right The odd one out amongst Rattin's Worldmasters is SH·15037, an LCRT1/1 of 1968 with C50D coachwork built in Italy by Desimon, almost certainly a unique combination of chassis and body (M. Fenton).

Centre right The origins of this Strachan-bodied Bedford SB are unknown. It may have been supplied new to Switzerland or perhaps acquired at second-hand from the British Armed Forces. The owner, C. Meyer & Sohne of Buchdruckerei, Jona, used it for the transportation of school children, hence the unusually high seating capacity for an SB of B51D (B.A. Tilley).

Bottom right Apart from a handful of Leyland Leopards bought by some French companies in the 1960s, the only other British-made vehicles supplied to any operator in the whole of France would seem to be the 11.3 m Leyland Nationals supplied to Dijon and St Etienne. Those at Dijon must have created a considerable impression for they were sold in 1975 after a mere two years of service to CFVE St Etienne in which fleet they became Nos 261-266, continuing the series commenced at 251 by St Etienne's own Nationals. 267 was another second-hand National, the Leyland (France) demonstrator followed, in 1977, by 268-277 — phase two Nationals making a grand total of 27 with this operator. No 253 (3341 RD 42) is illustrated *leaving* the Montreynaud terminus for the city despite information to the contrary displayed on the blind. It is not just in Britain where this happens! (M. Fenton).

THE ORIENT

When the Treaty of Nanking was drawn-up in 1842, Hong Kong was 80 sq km of virtually uninhabited island. By 1898 the colony included a number of additional islands as well as an area of mainland and had grown to its present size of a little over 1,000 sq km.

Above Bus services on Hong Kong Island are provided by the China Motor Bus Company Ltd, a company which commenced operation in the 1920s. During the 1950s CMB took delivery of many Guy Arab single-deckers, the illustrated example—HK 4212—being one of a small number of short wheelbase Gardner 5LW-engined Arab IVs with Metal Sections B30C bodies delivered in 1954 (D. Withers).

Left At about the same time as CMB Guys were entering service, Hong Kong's other large operator, the Kowloon Motor Bus Company (1933) Ltd, was busy buying large quantities of Daimler CVG5s with Metal Sections bodies. D124, HK 4325 is one of the 1956 batch with H32/27D seating, the Manchester style front being a later modification. KMB operate not only in Kowloon City but additionally in the area of the mainland known as the New Territories (D. Withers).

Right A total of 210 specially built 34 ft long AEC Regent V 2D2RA chassis were bought by KMB between 1963 and 1966. The first 30 had bodies by the British Aluminium Company but subsequent deliveries had Metal Sections bodies, these being assembled at KMB's Kwun Tong works. The dual door bodies on these buses vary slightly in capacity from batch to batch but AD 4876 is typical in having seats for 50 passengers upstairs, 34 seats downstairs and space for a further 42 standees in its Met-Sec body. This 1965 bus was evidently in need of some attention when photographed in Kowloon in 1970, to judge by the raised bonnet *(B.A. Tilley)*.

Centre right 100 Perkins V8-engined Seddon Pennine IVs with Seddon B47D bodies were delivered to KMB in 1970. After a short time in service, however, it became clear that these buses would provide many headaches for the company. Two problems in particular were associated with the bodies; grounding of the fibreglass front panel assembly and, more seriously, stresses concentrated in the weak area around the centre exit producing an unfortunate arching of the body. These difficulties, it must be said, were not the sole preserve of KMB's Seddons as some United Kingdom operators experienced similar misfortunes with two-door Seddon bodies on both Pennine IV and rear-engined RU chassis. Fires were another endearing feature of the type, apparently caused by the use of electrical wiring unsuitable for such a climate, at least eight buses being lost in this way. In order to overcome the problem of grounding many buses received new aluminium fronts of rather basic style like AR 7608, although the split roof panelling over the centre door and a severe droop in the rear half of the body suggest that more serious structural problems remained *(D. Withers)*.

Right City Buses was the name chosen for a new private hire bus company established in Hong Kong in 1979. Nearly all the company's initial purchases consisted of second-hand Daimler Fleetlines, D7 (CC 7217) being one of a trio of former West Midlands PTE CRG6/33 chassis with Park Royal bodywork dating from 1969, this particular vehicle having been WMPTE 3886, SOE 886H *(D.A. Lewis)*.

Above China Motor Bus Co DD1, BX 2164, appeared on the Hestair-Dennis stand at the 1978 Commercial Motor Show in the National Exhibition Centre, Birmingham. This impressive vehicle, the only one of its type so far with CMB, consists of a 10 m long, Gardner-engined Dennis Dominator DD113A chassis with a 104-seater (H62/42D) East Lancashire body *(A. Mortimer)*.

Macau, a small overseas province of Portugal, is situated on the western side of the wide Chu Chiang (Pearl River) estuary on the coast of southern China. It has an area of 16 sq km and a population of about ¼ million. The City of Macau is connected to the two offshore islands of Taipa and Coloane by a causeway completed in 1975. A ferry boat and hydrofoil service connects Macau with Hong Kong on the opposite side of the estuary some 65 km distant, the journey by hydrofoil taking a little over one hour.

Below 30 second-hand Bristol L5G buses were purchased by the Companhia de Autocarros Fok-Lei Lda over a ten-year period commencing in the mid-1950s. A little under half this number were of the original L type with a high mounted radiator produced from 1938 to 1942 as represented by L105, M-19-07. This veteran, which was nearing its fortieth birthday when photographed, was originally Southern National 306, DDV 33. It carries a Beadle body built in 1950 as B36R but rebuilt in Macau as B29D *(D. Withers)*.

Right The post-war L type is represented by L123, M-27-06, formerly LHN 805, one of six United L5Gs of 1949 exported in the mid-1960s. In Macau the rear entrance Eastern Coachworks body was rebuilt with an additional entrance — as B33D — and full depth sliding windows installed to provide adequate ventilation in the humid environment *(R. Gingell)*.

Right Following successful operation of L types, the underfloor-engined LS was taken into Tilling fleet ownership. The same pattern was repeated in Macau, although some 17 or 18 years behind schedule, ten LS5Gs being acquired by Fok-Lei between 1969 and 1974. M-58-23, which was formerly Bristol 2883, UHT 493, has an especially interesting history. It was built in 1952 but did not enter service until 1955, Bristol Commercial Vehicles using it in the meantime for experimental purposes. As built it had a two-stroke Commer TS3 engine which was retained until 1956 when a more orthodox Gardner 5HLW was fitted. The body is also worthy of note being built as B43D, a rare layout at that time, converted to a more normal B45F in 1962, reconverted to B43D in Macau and then rebuilt yet again to the illustrated form as B--T! As the practice of registration swapping is not unknown in Macau, it will come as no surprise for readers to learn that this LS once carried the registration M-53-81 prior to assuming its current identity, an ex-West Yorkshire Road Car Company LS being the original recipient of the registration M-58-23! *(D. Withers)*.

Right When the causeway to the islands of Taipa and Coloane was completed in 1975, 11 second-hand double-deckers were quickly acquired for use on the new routes, one of the first being CC203, M-87-58, a Daimler CCG6/Weymann of 1963 formerly Chesterfield Corporation 260, 3260 NU. It is here seen employed on service 21 to Coloane *(D. Withers)*.

Left In addition to the Singapore Traction Company several small private bus companies operated in the country until enforced mergers caused a cessation of their activities. One such operator was the Katong–Bedok Bus Service who, as the title implies, ran between the two places named. A number of Vulcans were owned by Katong-Bedok including SH 134, a 6PF of about 1950 which had central entrance bodywork by an unknown Singapore builder *(R.F. Mack)*.

Below left The island of Taiwan, once known by its Portuguese name of Formosa, measures approximately 380 km from north to south and is separated from the south-eastern coast of mainland, communist China by the 160 km wide Taiwan Kaikyo or Formosa Strait. An especially interesting vehicle seen at Chai-I in 1980 was 66-2429; a Volvo B57 with Willowbrook 008 Spacecar coachwork which was apparently assembled locally *(I.N. Lynas)*.

Below Due south of Taiwan in South-East Asia are the many islands which make up the Republic of the Philippines. Few vehicles with British-made chassis are to be found here apart from a number of Alexander-bodied Leyland Atlanteans operating in the capital, Manila, with the Metro Manila Transit Corporation. An especially interesting coach with a British connection was to be found in the Tourmaster Travel Service fleet in 1980 in the shape of a ckd Plaxton Supreme-bodied Japanese Mitsubishi Fuso rear-engined chassis! *(I.N. Lynas)*.

Right The small island state of Singapore with an area of just over 500 sq km lies at the southern end of the Malay peninsula and is connected to it by means of a causeway across the narrow Johore Strait. The country's main bus operator was for many years the English-owned Singapore Traction Company. Of the various British-made chassis bought by the STC, Albions were the most numerous with, for example, more than 200 Victors—mainly of the FT39 type—entering service in the late 1940s and early '50s. All had locally produced bodywork, the illustrated example, STC 126 being typical *(R.F. Mack)*.

Right Fok-Lei 210, M-07-14, one of two Bristol KSW6Gs in Macau, was formerly Bristol Omnibus Company C8431, YHT 927. Numerically this was Bristol's last K type, indeed only eight other KSWs had higher chassis numbers, all these going to Brighton, Hove & District in the same year— 1957. The front entrance, labelled it will be noted in Chinese, Portuguese and English was added on behalf of its new owner, the ECW body becoming H33/22D in this modified form. The other KSW6G, acquired from the same source, was not only converted to two-door layout but additionally rebuilt to open-top! *(D. Withers)*.

AUSTRALASIA

New Zealand consists of two main islands; North Island with an area of 115,000 sq km being a little smaller than England and South Island at 150,000 sq km a little larger. The total population is, however, very low at a shade over 3 million, mostly of British descent, North Island having the greater share with around 2 million. Not surprisingly, many British-made vehicles have operated in the country.

Below The largest city of North Island and, indeed, of New Zealand, is Auckland with a population of ¾ million. Bus services were provided by the Auckland Transport Board until 1964 when the operator became the Auckland Regional Authority. In the 1950s Saunders-roe bodies, supplied in knocked down form, were favoured with Daimler Freeline, Bedford SB and Leyland Royal Tiger chassis all receiving this attractively styled bodywork. The Leylands — 50 of the OPSU1/1 type — all came in 1953, No 499, EZ2636, being numerically the penultimate example *(B.A. Tilley)*.

Left The sole supplier of post-war Auckland trolleybus chassis was British United Traction (BUT), formed from pooling AEC and Leyland trolleybus activities in 1946. Initially vehicles of the 9711T model were purchased but RETB/1s then followed. No 31, EZ 2331, is of the earlier type, one of 14 Metro-Cammell-bodied 9711Ts delivered in 1951 *(B.A. Tilley)*.

Right The coastal city of Whangarei, 175 km to the north of Auckland, has bus services provided on the council's behalf by the Northern Motor Bus Company, an operator established in the 1920s. No 3 in the fleet was this AEC 7.7L-engined Dennis Lancet, chassis 148J3, one of the earliest of the small number of exported Lancet 3s. The B34F body on FX 1950 was built by a so far unidentified New Zealand firm *(B.A. Tilley)*.

Right The small North Island operator, J. Nimon & Sons Ltd of Havelock North, had two elderly petrol-engined Morris Commercial PP/R chassis with bodywork by Nuttall's of Napier, one of them, No 6, EM8606, dating from 1951 *(B.A. Tilley)*.

Below right The New Zealand capital, Wellington, situated on the southern tip of North Island has, like Auckland, both motor-bus and trolleybus services, the trolleys being the first in New Zealand commencing in 1924. Motor-bus operation in Wellington followed a course similar to many British municipal systems having its origins in the years around 1920 with the initial routes, essentially tramway feeders, being followed by a period of expansion. Of the rolling stock, AEC and Leyland buses proved popular, purchased almost to the exclusion of every other make, Leyland Leopards being the current choice. The illustration shows preserved Leyland OPS1 No 12, EV6799, one of four which entered service with Wellington Tramways, as it then was, in 1947-8, bodied, it is thought, by Wellington themselves *(B.A. Tilley)*.

Bottom right Eastbourne, as most readers will know, is a seaside resort especially popular with the elderly and, having its own municipal bus fleet. Eastbourne Borough Council 4, CQ1404, is a 1952 Harrington-bodied Dennis Falcon L6 demonstrator acquired in 1953. However, popping along the coast to the Harrington works at Hove or going up the road to the Dennis factory at Guildford for parts would have been a lengthy business for, despite the convincing description, this is Eastbourne, New Zealand, a few kilometres to the east of Wellington. After withdrawal from Eastbourne service in 1968 the Falcon winged its way to North Island independent Macfarlane's Passenger Transport of Te Aroha, Hamilton, who replaced the original Dennis oil engine with a Thames unit. When photographed in April 1974 it was in use as a school bus with Macfarlane's *(B.A. Tilley)*.

Above One of the most remarkable vehicles with a New Zealand operator must have been ES 9877, No 3 in the fleet of Martin Smith Motors Ltd of Masterton, North Island, for this 1934 Leyland Cub KP3 bodied by Crawley-Ridley was still in regular use when photographed in 1974! Just for good measure an even earlier Cub, a 1931 KP3, also with Crawley-Ridley bodywork, was at the same time still intact in the garage although no longer used in service *(B.A. Tilley)*.

Below The rear-engined Foden PVRF6 was represented in New Zealand by five of the last chassis built which were ordered by the Whenupai Bus Company of Auckland and bodied by Hawke Brothers of Takinini. At least four, and possibly all five, of these interesting vehicles were later acquired by the Hawke's Bay Motor Company Ltd of Napier, North Island, a company which in turn was taken over by Mount Cook Landlines. Photographed shortly after the take-over was Hawke's Bay C5, EN6952, which was based on chassis 33864, new in 1955 *(B.A. Tilley)*.

Above The city of Dunedin, capital of Otago Province, South Island, was founded in 1848 as a Scottish Free Church settlement, its name being derived from Duneideann, the Gaelic name for Edinburgh. Almost every conceivable form of public transport has appeared on the streets of Dunedin with steam trams, horse trams, electric trams, cable cars, trolleybuses and motor-buses all being used at some time. The trolleybus routes, introduced as late as December 1950, reached their peak in the early 1960s and then, from 1967, declined steadily although closure, scheduled for 1976, was postponed for a few years due mainly to a fuel shortage. Despite No 10, DK 3158, being one of the earliest of Dunedin's trolleys, a 1951 BUT RETB/1 bodied by New Zealand Motor Bodies, it was still surviving in 1976 and, indeed, was expected to remain in service to the end of the system. This interesting shot proves that the famous pram hooks are used for this purpose and makes the author wonder whether a harassed mother has ever forgotten to remove her infant from his push chair and consequently given the little fellow an unexpectedly exhilarating ride! *(B.A. Tilley)*.

Below The Gisborne Municipal Bus Service of North Island operated this ex-demonstration Mulliner-bodied Seddon Mk 6 from the mid-1950s until about 1969, when it was sold to Finley of Taupo. A little later the Seddon and the rest of the Finley fleet were acquired by the Hawke's Bay Motor Company of Napier, this shot being taken soon after its acquisition. In keeping with most New Zealand buses of its time, several different registrations were carried by the Seddon as re-registration every 5 years was the law until permanent registrations began to be issued from 1964. When new, as Gisborne No 1, it carried the registration P 1208, becoming P 1119 when first re-registered, and then finally becoming EM2195 *(B.A. Tilley)*.

Left Dunedin Corporation Transport's first underfloor-engined buses were six AH470-engined MU3RAE model AEC Reliances with 36-seat Park Royal bodywork delivered in 1955, vehicles which would, of course, have been quite at home in any of a host of British fleets. No 106, DK 3223, lasted until 1976 when, along with several other Reliances, it was replaced by an Emslie-bodied Leyland Leopard PSU3 *(B.A. Tilley).*

Left This former Dunedin bus with bodywork built in the undertaking's own workshops, originally as FB35D, was one of four dating from the early 1950s all based on the AEC Regal III 9621E chassis. After withdrawal from service No 54 avoided the scrap merchants as it was bought for preservation in the Motor Coach Museum, Wellington, the location of this photograph *(B.A. Tilley).*

Left The local firm Emslie Consolidated Industries built their first ever bus bodies on a batch of ten Leyland Panther PSUR1B/1R chassis for Dunedin between 1970 and early 1972, No 148, DP6432, entering service in July 1971 *(B.A. Tilley).*

Right The frequently used description of Christchurch being 'the most English city outside England' could have been devised with the bus man in mind, for the Christchurch Transport Board bought 95 AEC Regal IVs of the 9821E model in the years 1952-4, 56 of which had Park Royal bodywork with the remainder, like 316, DV427, having attractive Crossley bodies. Surprisingly, although Crossley bodies were popular on AECs in the United Kingdom, not one Regal IV received a body of this make for the home market. Park Royal-bodied AEC Reliances, which followed the Regals and Bristol RELLs with ckd Eastern Coachworks bodies delivered in the 1970s, have done little to dispel the English image of this attractive city *(B.A. Tilley)*.

Right Mount Cook, at 3,763 m the highest mountain in New Zealand, lends its name to the Christchurch-based touring fleet Mount Cook Landlines. Bedfords have regularly featured in the fleet, including VALs and SBs, the illustrated vehicle, No 208 'Mount Goldsmith', being a 1971 NZMB-bodied YRQ, one of the first examples of this model in the country. It was photographed at Queenstown, South Island, on tour work in 1974 *(B.A. Tilley)*.

Right Of the very large number of Bedford SBs exported, more than 2,000 were sold to New Zealand operators, the relatively cheap purchase price and low running costs making the SB an attractive proposition to operators. ER 9698, No 18 in the fleet of Madge Motors of Palmerston North, North Island, is an early example of the marque dating from 1952 and bodied by the now defunct Crawley-Ridley concern of Christchurch *(B.A. Tilley)*.

Above A large percentage of the Bedford SBs sold to New Zealand companies had the 300 cu in Bedford petrol engine, the SB3 variant. Very unusual indeed, though, is the combination of an SB3 chassis and raised deck New Zealand Motor Bodies coachwork, Cunningham's of Oamaru, South Island, having this rare bird, EZ 9399, which was delivered in 1963 *(B.A. Tilley)*.

Australia is a vast country having an area of 7.7 million sq km—more than 30 times greater than that of the United Kingdom—but yet a population of only 14 million, most of whom are concentrated in the south between Brisbane and Adelaide. Where there are people there are buses and it is therefore not surprising that the states of New South Wales, Victoria and the southern part of Queensland provide the lion's share of material.

Below A total of 67 Leyland Tiger OPS1 chassis were purchased by the Melbourne & Metropolitan Tramways Board in the early post-war period, some being bodied by the board themselves with others like 415, ET·415 of 1949 receiving bodywork by the large Commonwealth Engineering concern of Granville, New South Wales. The OPS1 differed from the home market PS1 in that it had a standard width of 8 ft rather than 7 ft 6 in and received the pre-war 8.6L engine in place of the PS1's smaller 7.4L E181 unit *(B.A. Tilley)*.

28

Right The Leyland Panther, which was quite popular for some time in Australia, was bodied by several firms including Denning, although of the many Panthers dealt with by this Queensland builder, only four had coach bodies. Three were of the style exemplified by US Coach Lines of Belgrave, Victoria No 89 KPR 889, which had a PSUR1A/2RT chassis and was new in 1970, the same year that it was photographed (B.A. Tilley).

Right Tomaino's Coach Lines of Myrtleford, Victoria IVQ 167 is one of two Bedford VAL70s with Belgian-built Van Hool coachwork imported by Pyke's Tours of Sydney in 1971. It passed with the Pyke business to Australian Accommodated Tours and was then sold to Tomaino for use on school and charter work. It was photographed in 1980 (B.A. Tilley).

Below right This 33 ft long AEC, originally operated by Reid's Bus Service of Northcote, has the distinction of being the only Regal III supplied new to a private operator in the state of Victoria. The similarity in appearance between this bus and the many Melbourne & Metropolitan Tramways Board Regals of the early 1950s is easily explained for it was treated as an additional vehicle in a batch being bodied in 1953 for that operator by Martin & King of Malvern. When photographed, in 1964, the Regal had become No 2, GCP 809, in the fleet of another Victoria private operator; the Portsea Passenger Service of Sorrento (B.A. Tilley).

Above GMF·583 represents a make rarely found in Australia namely Seddon. I.J. Cook & Son of Geelong, Victoria, were the owners of this Mark 4 which had bodywork complete with wheel spats by the small but old-established builder Cheetham & Borwick of Carlton *(B.A. Tilley)*.

Below The only Leyland Atlanteans new to Australia were the 224 supplied between 1969 and 1972 to the Public Transport Commission, Sydney, which had H39/27D bodies by the Pressed Metal Corporation (PMC). Because of union opposition to one-man operation of double-deckers, and a poor reliability record, many of these buses were sold after quite short periods of service, the first withdrawals taking place in 1978. PTC No 1126, ⊕ 1126, a PDR1A/1 of 1971, went north to the Newcastle area and Fellowe's Bus Service of Swansea, with whom it became ⊕ 762 *(B.A. Tilley)*.

Above A total of 143 SPCX19W Albion Venturers entered service with the Department of Road Transport & Tramways in the years 1947-9. When new all had dual-door bodywork, H33/26D, but between 1962 and 1968 most had their front doors removed. This later, rebuilt form is demonstrated by MO·5223, here shown in private ownership with Guilfoyle of Scone, New South Wales. The body is by Commonwealth Engineering although identical bodies were also constructed by Clyde Engineering (B.A. Tilley).

Below MO·3461 is a 1950 Gardner 4LK-engined Guy Otter with B36F bodywork by Syd Wood of Bankstown, owned by the Grafton Bus Company of Grafton, New South Wales (B.A. Tilley).

Left This Leyland Panther Cub PSRC1/1 which was new in 1964 as Manchester Corporation 62, ANF 162B, had an illustrious start to its career being exhibited at that year's Earls Court Commercial Motor Show. Some eight years later it was working in Australia for the Toronto Bus Service from the town of the same name in New South Wales, its Park Royal body having been neatly rebuilt from B43D to B47F (B.A. Tilley).

Left A consignment of 42 Leyland Olympic EL2/44s was written off in October 1964 when the East German ship *Magdeburg*, which was taking them from Dagenham to Cuba, heeled over and became partially submerged in the Thames following collision with the Japanese cargo vessel *Yamashiro Maru* in thick fog off Broadness Point. The Bosnjak Bus Group from Sydney acquired a number of salvaged Olympics and used the units from seven of them in locally-made chassis which then received CVI (Commercial Vehicle Industries) B49D bodies. The Parramatta Bus Company, part of the Bosnjak group, operated all seven including ^m_o 5497 of 1969, as well as one complete Metro-Cammell bodied Olympic which had been rebuilt to right hand drive (B.A. Tilley).

Left The Hume Street South Bus Service of Toowoomba, Queensland, still had this 1946 Bedford OB in service in the late 1970s its body being made by the quaintly named builder, Grice (B.A. Tilley).

Above The old established company Dion's Bus Service of Fairymeadow is one of several private operators serving the industrialised city of Wollongong. Dion's ᵐ 6054 is a pre-selective Guy Arab III 6LW/Properts B41D dating from 1953, which was inherited with the business of another Wollongong operator Price of Austinmer. For readers outside Australia the difference between the New South Wales ᵐ and MO numbers should be explained; the former being Metropolitan issue, ie, the cities of Sydney, Wollongong and Newcastle, and the latter MO series being country issue. In some cases the two series overlap and there are also a few fleets in outer areas of the three cities which have mixed ᵐ and MO registered stock *(B.A. Tilley)*.

Below All four Foden double-deckers which ran in Australia were fitted with standard H33/26D Commonwealth Engineering bodywork, however, both of the Punchbowl Bus Company's vehicles were later rebodied as single-deckers on extended chassis. Subsequently one of this pair, which had 1960 Comeng 41 seat bodywork on its 1948 PVD6 chassis passed to another New South Wales private operator Kaiser of Matcham with whom it became MO·4833 *(B.A. Tilley)*.

Above Some truly amazing vehicles were operated by the now ceased Black & White fleet of Sandgate, Queensland. For example, owned at the time operations finished in 1974 were sundry single-deck rebodied Leyland TD5s, one of the few AEC Sabres built, a Royal Tiger with an ex-Brisbane trolleybus body and, from the same source, the strangest vehicle of all, an Athol Hedges-bodied Sunbeam MF2B trolleybus powered by a Leyland 0.680 diesel! A little earlier, in 1965, this impressive Foden also formed part of the fleet, a 33 ft PVSC6 with raised deck coachwork by Lawton—of South Australia it should be stressed and not Staffordshire, England *(B.A. Tilley)*.

Below It is not generally realised how popular early post-war Commers were in the export market for of almost 1,000 Avenger Is produced in the years 1948 to 1952, more than one third were exported. This Australian Avenger I, bodied by Watt Bros of Brisbane, operated for its entire working life in the state of Queensland as Ipswich–Amberley–Rosewood Bus Service 15. For completeness its Queensland registration was Q586.600 and its PSV licence number Q/tp 1698, although neither is being displayed in this shot *(B.A. Tilley)*.

Above A total of 36 Cummins V6-engined Daimler Roadliners were sold to the municipal Tramways Trust, Adelaide, South Australia in 1969, 35 of which received 2.6 m (8 ft 6 in) wide Freighter Industries B46D bodies as MTT Nos 201-235. The thirty-sixth chassis was bought specifically as a source of spare parts, this unusual practice having been standard in Adelaide for many years *(B.A. Tilley)*.

Below This Syd Wood-bodied Atkinson, registered 449·551, was new in 1955 with another similar vehicle to the Cole Bus Service although, by the time this shot was taken at Klemzig in 1963, it had passed to another private operator in the state of South Australia, Slattery's Bus Service of Payneham. Most of the small number of Atkinsons sold to Australian companies had purpose-built underfloor-engined PSV chassis but a few, like the Slattery bus, used the Gardner 4LK engined forward control truck chassis, the L644L model *(B.A. Tilley)*.

ISLANDS IN THE SUN

The Canary Islands, which are situated off the north-western coast of Africa, form part of metropolitan Spain just as the island of Madeira to the north of the Canaries is a part of Portugal. West of Madeira, and about one third of the way across the Atlantic, are the nine islands which comprise the Azores, a group which is also part of Portugal.

Sociedade de Automoveis da Madeira Lda (SAM) was one of the earliest companies in the world to operate Seddon buses, with two Mark 5s entering service in 1947. The Mark 5 was really a 13 ft 6 in wheelbase truck chassis but, nevertheless, further vehicles of this type were bought until purpose-built passenger chassis became available from Seddon. LH-16-38, illustrated, is one of the first few Mark 4s bought by SAM and, although it may seem unlikely, it has a body by Seddon. The distinctly un-Seddon appearance stems from the fact that a completely new front has been fitted by SAM and the traditional rectangular radiator removed, possibly as a result of accident damage *(M. Fenton)*.

Above The underfloor-engined Seddon Mark 19 was a peculiar hybrid employing an AEC AH410 engine and AEC gearbox. It was a rare beast, especially in the United Kingdom where just one Harrington-bodied example was sold — VHO 200. Overall about 30 chassis were constructed in the period 1959-61, ten of which are known to have been exported to Madeira, the lion's share of eight chassis going to SAM. Included in this total is MA-40-49 which has a 42-seat central entrance body built by SAM's associated company Leacock to Alfredo Caetano design in 1962. In later years Leacock bodies were built to UTIC design *(M. Fenton)*.

Below Empresa Automobilista de São Martinho Lda (EASML) is a small Madeiran operator closely associated with the large SAM concern. Rolling stock delivered to EASML in the past 20 years consisted entirely of UTIC-AEC integral buses but a few earlier more interesting buses are still used. In this category is MA-25-53 a 1950 Morris Commercial OP/L with Leacock bodywork constructed in the 1960s. The Morris OP/L (Oil Passenger Left) was the left-hand drive version of the more familiar OP/R chassis which attracted a limited following in the period 1948-52 in the United Kingdom *(M. Fenton)*.

37

Left Two outwardly similar normal control Commers entered service with Empresa de Automoveis do Caniço Lda (EACL) in 1950. MA-25-77 is a Commando of the P30A export series produced between 1949 and 1952. The body was built by the now defunct Madeiran builder Jacinto Vicina Gomes. Twin bus MD-25-59 also had a Gomes body but on the Q4 4/5-ton chassis, the goods equivalent of the Commando which was in production at the same time. Both were still regular performers in July 1979 working mainly from Funchal, the main town on Madeira, to Caniço *(M. Fenton)*.

Left Although a Leyland Leopard badge is proudly carried by Sociedade de Automoveis de São Roque do Faial (SASRF) 30, MD-42-49, it is in fact not a PSU3 or a PSU4 or any other variety of Leopard! The chassis is one of three Royal Tiger Cubs in the fleet dating from 1963-4. The unusual but stylish Salvador Caetano central entrance body is enhanced by the attractive grey, red and white livery chosen by SASRF, a company which, in the author's view, is probably the smartest in Madeira. The Royal Tiger Cub badge, which is a combination of the enamelled head from a Tiger Cub badge mounted on a Leopard type shield, must have been in permanently short supply at Leyland's as the author has seen Royal Tiger Cubs which have had from new either ordinary Tiger Cub badges or Royal Tiger badges besides this Leopard version *(M. Fenton)*.

Left SAM showed great loyalty to Seddon in purchasing buses based on Marks 4, 5, 6, 7, 10, 17 and 19 chassis from 1947 to 1962. Several years then elapsed before the next Seddon chassis arrived in the fleet in the shape of four Pennine IVs acquired in the late 1960s and early '70s. MD-54-10, at the time of writing, is SAM's newest Seddon, a Pennine IV bodied by Alfredo Caetano in 1971. Although further purchase of Seddons by SAM appears unlikely, such a move cannot be ruled out as one of the other Madeiran operators, Rodoeste, recently took delivery of a UTIC-bodied Pennine VII following ten Seddon-less years *(M. Fenton)*.

Above São Miguel island has both the largest area and largest population (approximately 120,000) of the Azores. It also has three bus operators although, unlike Madeira, the variety of makes is rather limited, especially for the enthusiast of British-made buses. Varela & Companhia Lda, however, have a handful of specimens worthy of attention including the five buses used on urban services in Ponta Delgada the chief town of São Miguel. These remarkably unattractive buses have second-hand, home-made bodies transferred from their original chassis to new Austin FG K100 5-ton goods chassis in the late 1960s. AR-61-15, whose standard of upkeep is definitely non-typical of the Varela fleet, was photographed in Ponta Delgada in July 1979 *(M. Fenton)*.

Below No, not a Mercedes-Benz but an AEC Monocoach! The Monocoach of integral construction was popular with many Portuguese operators during the years 1955 to 1958, UTIC usually building the bodies. A small number of UTIC-bodied Monocoaches was exported to São Miguel with all three operators still having operational examples in 1979. The sole representative of the marque in the Auto Viacão Michaelense fleet was the illustrated AR-28-81 which had been fitted with a *front mounted* Mercedes engine and gearbox. A Mercedes Monocoach perhaps? *(M. Fenton)*.

Above Probably the best known bus operator in the island of Gran Canaria, in the Canary Islands, was the yellow liveried AICASA fleet or, to give it its full title, Autobuses Interurbanos Canarios SA, which ceased trading in the early 1970s. Following the operation of some very early Daimlers, the company then purchased a small number of new Daimler CVD6 chassis in the late 1940s and early '50s. Later on, between 1954 and 1962, over 60 Daimler CVD6s were acquired from a variety of sources along with a few COG5s and CW series chassis. Most of these acquisitions continued with their original British coachwork, converted for operation on the right-hand side of the road by the rebuilding of the old offside emergency exit as the new entrance. GC-10971 can be seen with its Burlingham body so converted in this view taken in Las Palmas in 1961. It was new in 1948, as FJW 329, to one of Everall's associated companies Moore's Motor Services of Wombourn, Wolverhampton. In 1956 the vehicle was taken into Everall ownership when the Moore fleet was absorbed by its parent company. After a few months with Everall it was exported to the Canaries finally entering service in 1957 with AICASA *(M. Dryhurst).*

Left Many Seddon Mark 4s were bodied by small coachbuilders in the hectic post-war period with some exceptionally interesting and rare specimens resulting. The only known Scunthorpe Motors-bodied Seddon Mark 4 was HFU 335 which was new in 1950 to Portman Coaches of the same town. By 1961 it had emigrated to Gran Canaria and, suitably rebuilt as B28D and re-registered GC-16966, operated for about ten more years with the Asociación Patronal de Jardineras Guagas *(M. Dryhurst).*

Above Not all the Daimlers acquired by AICASA had coachwork by well known companies, some being of extremely dubious quality having been constructed during the early post-war boom period when good quality seasoned timber for body framing was almost unobtainable. One cannot help but think that British operators knew exactly what they were disposed of when they sold relatively young vehicles to dealers and that equally AICASA did not know too much about the smaller UK coachbuilders. Of these, one of the least likely in the late 1940s was the Bridlington-based company Yorkshire Yachtbuilders! As the title implies the company's original business was not connected with road transport at all; a fact readily supported by the troubles operators had with this firm's bodies. One operator in Lancashire must have had some misgivings very soon after collecting his Yorkshire Yacht-bodied Daimler as the passenger door parted company with the rest of the body before the coach had left the East Riding! Presumably the body shops of AICASA must have worked miracles as Yorkshire Yacht-bodied GC-10438, formerly SML 475 of 1948, survived for several years following its acquisition in 1957 *(M. Dryhurst)*.

Right The Transportes Guanarteme fleet, although not comprising as many vehicles as some of the other Gran Canarian operators, nevertheless purchased its fair share of second-hand gems in the 1950s and 1960s. For example, in 1961 the company purchased three out of the four Willowbrook-bodied, double-deck Leyland Tigers which had been built for Birch Bros some ten years earlier. This unique batch had fully fronted, forward entrance bodywork on special 8 ft wide × 26 ft long PS1/4 chassis. In Gran Canaria the bodies were rebuilt with 'offside' central entrances although the original entrance may be clearly discerned in this shot of GC-17245, formerly Birch Bros K223, LXV 223 *(M. Dryhurst)*.

Left From the enthusiast's point of view, Tenerife was never as interesting as Gran Canaria although some second-hand ex-UK buses did operate there. For instance the Unión de Autobuses de Tenerife fleet contained a number of former Northern General Beadle-AEC chassisless vehicles from the 1953 DCN registered batch, Northern General Nos 1483-1492 *(M. Dryhurst)*.

Left Metalcraft bodied five Fodens of the advanced two-stroke, rear-engined PVRF6 model in 1951, to the order of Global Tours of London W1. The solitary example of this quintet which came to the Canary Islands in 1962 was used as a non-PSV with La Tropical Cerveza, a brewery. Ironically, although all the second-hand buses bought for public use in Gran Canaria required new entrances on the Spanish nearside, GC-20246 already had a full height entrance on that side, a legacy of its overseas touring work with Global *(M. Dryhurst)*.

Left GC-18517, No 15 in the Transportes Guanarteme fleet, seems to have led a schizophrenic existence as it is known to have run also as GC-18157. This former Tillings Transport coach, although having much of a Bristol look about it, is in fact a pre-war AEC Regal 0662 rebodied with a 1951 Eastern Coachworks body which in Gran Canaria had a central entrance on the right-hand side *(M. Dryhurst)*.

Above TF-14302 is a perfect mirror image of the type of coach found with a number of British independents in the early 1960s for it is a Duple Corinthian-bodied Commer Avenger IV of 1961. The Transportes de Tenerife fleet contained a relatively large number of Commers of Marks III and IV purchased between 1954 and 1965 with either Duple coachwork or bodywork built in the TTSL workshops at La Laguna *(M. Dryhurst).*

Many changes have taken place in Maltese bus operation since 1973 when the well known and well liked individual route colours disappeared. Green buses are now found almost everywhere, many second-hand units have ousted some old favourites and a re-registration scheme has been implemented. Cheap fares remain, though, and sufficient interesting buses still operate to make a visit worthwhile.

Below Malta 2820, since re-registered A.2820.M, is one of ten Bedford OWB chassis supplied soon after the end of the war in 1945, these OWBs being numbered amongst the last of the type to be built. The 32-seat body was made on the island by Zammit of Hamrun, an old-established builder now no longer making bodies. When photographed in 1974, 2820 was wearing the short lived Group C livery of red and white, one of three liveries which had replaced the old route colours in the previous year *(M. Fenton).*

Left Many ex-military vehicles found their way into the hands of Maltese bus operators in the late 1940s. The 4-ton Commer Q4 4X2 truck chassis was a popular choice for passenger use both in Malta and in the UK as it was almost identical to the contemporary Commando passenger chassis. At least eight Q4s were fitted with bus bodywork in Malta, that on 3310 being made by Joseph Brincat of Paola *(M. Fenton)*.

Left This Austin CXB/Aquilina photographed in Mellieha in 1975 was new in 1950 and, appropriately, worked the Mellieha service for many years prior to the reorganisation in 1973. In keeping with a large proportion of Maltese buses, a Bedford front axle has been fitted and a Leyland 0.370 engine has replaced 2750's original unit *(M. Fenton)*.

Below Zammit-bodied 2825, a Leyland Comet ECPO1, the only normal control Comet in Malta, entered service in the early 1950s. This splendid machine photographed at Zurrieq in 1974 was used only sporadically in its latter years before being finally withdrawn in 1977 *(M. Fenton)*.

Above However unlikely it may seem to the reader, 856 has beneath its Maltese-built Barbara body of 1961, a Leyland Tiger TS7 chassis of 1937 formerly Lincolnshire Road Car Co 472, FW 8825. The author recalls the day in 1974 in Valletta when he was approached by a man claiming to be the driver of a '1937 Leyland Tiger'. This claim was treated with some degree of scepticism as the vehicle in question, 856, was clearly a Bedford SB. However, once the chassis had been seen and the chassis plate inspected the author, by now rather grubby, was convinced of the authenticity of this claim *(M. Fenton)*.

Below Second-hand bus and coach chassis continued to be exported to Malta throughout the 1960s and 1970s. 4398 of Sultana, Gzira, consists of a 1957 AEC Reliance MU3RV chassis which formerly ran as Maidstone & District YKR 234 paired with a 1975 Aquilina body, one of the last built by the company. As may be seen from the illustration, extensive use has been made of Duple components *(M. Fenton)*.

SCANDINAVIAN SELECTION

British-made buses are still being purchased in moderate numbers by companies in Denmark and Finland, but they seem likely to become a thing of the past in Norway and Sweden in the not too distant future.

Below left Denmark has proved to be a steady market for British-made PSVs, especially those from the Leyland group. In the 1960s Tiger Cub, Worldmaster and Leopard chassis were all sold in the country mostly bodied by Dansk Automobil Byggeri, Leyland's Danish associate, a company better known as DAB. DV 96 356 is a Worldmaster LCRT1/1 of 1967 with DAB B41D bodywork in the fleet of Aage Iversen of Resdal, a small village in Jutland only a few km from the DAB factory at Silkeborg *(M. Fenton).*

Bottom left Exchange rates favourable to the Danes in the mid-1970s enabled bus operators in Denmark to purchase brand new Plaxton-bodied Fords or Bedfords for relatively modest sums of kroner. This attractive little 28-seat Bedford VAS5, which dates from 1977, was being used by Jørgen Pedersen of Sandager on his Assens to Middelfart stage service when photographed in September 1979 *(M. Fenton).*

Above right This Roe-bodied Daimler CVD6 is one of three double-deckers purchased in 1949 for evaluation by the Danish State Railways (DSB), an all-Leyland PD2 (KB 78 431) and a Guy Arab III (K24424) with Northern Counties bodywork completing the trio. Although these buses were of different makes they were all similar in respect of having right-hand drive and highbridge, rear entrance bodywork with platform doors *(Unknown).*

Centre right BB 90 028 is one of a small number of 6MU2LA AEC Reliances bodied by DAB for Danish operators in the early 1970s, this particular example entering service in 1970 with De Blaa Busser of Skive. The use of Leyland lettering in addition to the familiar AEC triangle is noteworthy, although a more unusual feature common to several Reliances cannot be seen in this view; namely the strange positioning of the Monocontrol gear-change unit, for it is rotated through 90 degrees and mounted on the right-hand side of the steering column making the change from first to second or third to fourth gear a lateral rather than vertical action! *(M. Fenton).*

Right Trolleybuses no longer run in Denmark, the last company with them being NESA, the North Zealand Electricity & Tramway Company or, for those conversant with Danish, Nordsjællands Elektricitets & Sporvejs Aktieselskab. Fleet No 31 (AH 79 531) photographed in Copenhagen in 1971 was one of 20 BUT LETB/1 chassis with Smit, Mygind & Muttemeier B30D + 35 bodies supplied to NESA in 1953 *(B.A. Tilley).*

Left CN 98 567, a rear-engined Magirus Deutz TR 140 has one of the few Plaxton Viewmaster bodies built for the Danish market. The impressive coach is one of three 12 m long Plaxton-bodied Magirus bought by Leif Nielsen of Strøby, although the first one, a 230R120 chassis with Supreme coachwork, was sold in 1979 after three years of service to Nymand of Nykøbing. At the time of the author's visit in September of that year a rare 12 m Bedford YMT/Plaxton Supreme was also owned by Nielsen *(M. Fenton)*.

Left Following the export success of Plaxton's in Denmark, Duple soon embarked upon a similar course offering the attractive Dominant body mounted on Ford chassis ranging from the shortened (8 m) R1014 chassis via the R1014 proper to the R1114. ER 94 928, a Dominant II-bodied R1014 had only been in service for a few months when photographed in 1979 with Herluf Poulson, a small operator in the north-west of Jutland based on the town of Hurup *(M. Fenton)*.

Left Coachwork by J. Ørum-Petersen of Herning is carried by BR 98 559, a petrol-engined Bedford SB3 of 1960. By the time this photograph was taken the SB, which was well into its twentieth year, was no longer in public service although it was still in regular use with a driving school at Køge near Copenhagen *(M. Fenton)*.

Above With the change over to driving on the right, in September 1967, Sweden required large numbers of new buses to augment those which had been converted for further service. Stockholm Tramways (Stockholms Sparvägar) placed orders for left-hand drive buses with several manufacturers including Leyland who supplied 200 Panther PSUR1/1Ls with Park Royal bodies. Actually 202 Stockholm Panthers were constructed as, initially, Leyland built a right-hand drive demonstrator in 1964, a vehicle instrumental in securing the order. This was followed in 1966 by a mirror image left-hand drive version which was exhibited at the Geneva Motor Show in 1967. By the time this shot was taken in 1980 only 30 or so of the batch remained in a serviceable condition with SL (Storstockholms Lokaltrafik) as it is now known, 4467, CHX 277 being numbered amongst the survivors. Both demonstrators are still extant at the time of writing; the right-hand drive version in the ownership of the well known Australian independent Forest Coachlines of Belrose, Sydney, and the left-hand drive example now converted to single-door layout, with a water ski team in Walsall, West Midlands *(M. Fenton)*.

Below The Swedish company Linjebuss of Gothenburg had various permutations of Park Royal-bodied AECs delivered in 1951-2, the bus illustrated being one of 24 long wheelbase 9821E model Regal IVs. Other Regal IVs with Park Royal bodies in this fleet included some similar single-door buses and coaches as well as a handful of short wheelbase two-door buses. Several more Regal IVs were bought by Linjebuss at about the same time in chassis form and bodied in Sweden by Aktiebolaget Svenska Järnvägsverkstäderna of Linköping, a company which mercifully traded under the initials ASJ! The front of one of these buses can just be seen peeping out from behind Park Royal-bodied 433, O 996 in this June 1956 view *(J. Humphrey)*.

Left 50 Leyland Atlanteans with two-door Park Royal bodies entered service in Stockholm in 1967 at the same time as the more numerous Panthers. Due to various problems, notably their excessive weight, these 11 m long giants had comparatively short lives with SL being withdrawn, together with their German-built Bussing contemporaries, after some eight or nine years of use. Three Atlanteans, however, evaded the scrap man's torch with one remaining in the capital for preservation and another going to a company in Gothenburg. The third operates during the summer months in Malmköping, a small town some 80 km west of Stockholm, the home of Sweden's equivalent of the Crich tramway museum *(M. Dryhurst)*.

Left JCG 912, No 250 in the fleet of Södermanlands Läns Trafik AB of Eskilstuna, is one of a pair of Duple-bodied Volvo B58/60 chassis sent to Sweden in 1976 by Moseley's in the hope of securing orders in that country. The bodies, which were a modified form of the Dominant, were constructed to comply with Swedish regulations and had a number of Scandinavian features such as heated mirrors and double glazing. Unfortunately orders did not materialise and the two remain as the only known examples of coaches with British-built bodies in the whole of Sweden *(M. Fenton)*.

Right Visitors to Finland by sea usually travel via Sweden and arrive at the port of Turku. One of the first sights to greet the visitor might be one of the town's mustard and cream liveried municipal buses, indeed the depot is only a few hundred metres from the ferry terminal. Seen at that depot in 1980 was Turku 19, TPZ·12, one of six low frame, 11 m LCRT1/1 Leyland Worldmasters of 1964 with locally built Nummela B27D + 32 bodies *(M. Fenton)*.

Right Of all the British-built buses found in Finland, Leylands are the most likely make to be seen with the Leopard being especially popular. Strangely, although all Finnish Leopards seem to have the designation PSU3, many are 12 m chassis, including Autokori-bodied HKK·616 of Valkeakosken Likenne Oy of Valkeakoski, which is officially a PSU3A/2L of 1971 *(M. Fenton)*.

Right Auto Arvela Oy is a medium-sized operator based on the small town of Somero midway between Turku and Helsinki. About half the fleet is of Leyland manufacture, including 52, TKU·752, a 1977 PSU3C/2L Leopard which has 47-seat Lahden Autokori (Lahti) bodywork *(M. Fenton)*.

Left Bus services in the town of Jyväskylä, some 250 km north of Helsinki, are provided by the company Jyväskylän Likenne Oy using a mixture of Scandinavian and British-built rolling stock. In the latter category is No 114, XCU·914, one of several Ford R1114 chassis with Ajokki of Tampere standee bodywork delivered in the late 1970s. Additionally JL has a number of slightly earlier R1114s with English-sounding Boxer bodies, some of which are unusually equipped with Leyland pneumocyclic gearboxes and two-pedal control! *(M. Fenton).*

Left Because of the many unmetalled secondary roads found in Finland, rear-engined buses with their low frames and vulnerable engines are usually restricted to urban services. In view of this it is not surprising that the Leyland Panther had but a limited following in the country with only Turku municipality and a handful of independents buying examples. One of the few Panthers to last until the 1980s was Koiviston Auto Oy IRY·20, a Wiima-bodied PSUR1/1L of 1968 photographed in Lahti on a scorching July day in 1980. Contrary to what many people think, Finnish summers are often very hot with temperatures sometimes reaching 30 degrees C. Would-be campers should also note that ferocious mosquitoes can be a problem in the vicinity of Finland's many lakes *(M. Fenton).*

Left Three Norwegian operators purchased virtually identical 10.9 m, two-door Leyland Nationals, although these vehicles as a whole had minor variations from the standard Leyland product in, for example, the provision of electrically-heated windscreens. Several were bought for use in the port of Kristiansand with the enthusiastic Leyland user Vaagsbygd Ruta, but the rest ran in the capital, Oslo, with Oslo Sporveier taking three in 1974 and the private operator Schoyens Bilcentraler acquiring 12 in the same year, one of these being DB52410, No 108 in the Schoyens fleet *(M. Fenton).*

Right The Kristiansand operator Vaagsbygd Ruta has for some years been a regular customer of the body-builder Brodrene Repstads Karrosserifabrikk (BRK) of nearby Søgne, this Leyland Panther PSUR1A/1L of 1969 illustrating the type of bodywork BRK were producing at that time. For a while the Panther was quite popular with Vaagsbygd Ruta but by 1980 No 3, K·3063 had become the last operational example with the company, although British interest was maintained in the fleet in the shape of BRK-bodied Leyland Worldmasters and Leyland Nationals *(M. Fenton)*.

Right Although British-made buses are now rare in Norway, Kristiansand has the luxury of two Leyland operators for, in addition to Vaagsbygd Ruta, the smaller Bybussen company also has Leylands; a pair of 1967 LCRT1/1 Worldmasters with BRK B37T + 20 bodies *(M. Fenton)*.

Right At the time of writing the only place in Norway where trolleybuses may be found in operation is the attractive city of Bergen although, sadly, Bergens Sporvei no longer use British-built stock, the present fleet consisting mainly of some rather old-fashioned looking Czech-built Skodas and a number of newer and very smart Volvos. One of the earlier, and now withdrawn, vehicles was 0·5623 a Munck-bodied Sunbeam of 1957 which was photographed in 1964 at the Natlandsveien terminus. In the summer of 1980 two derelict Sunbeams were still extant at the nearby trolleybus garage, the intention being that one of them would eventually be preserved *(W. A. Camwell)*.

FROM PMT & SUT...

Over the years many buses from former British Electric Traction group fleets have been exported for further service in a variety of differing environments.

The ten Daimler CVD6/Burlingham buses delivered to Potteries Motor Traction (PMT) in 1948, LVT 691-700, seem to have been quite a gregarious bunch with all ten continuing in service until 1961 at which time all were withdrawn! Six of them stayed together and were exported to Gran Canaria, one of the Canary Islands of the North Atlantic, and the fleet of AICASA where they entered service in 1962 after suitable rebuilding with new entrances, GC-20823 having been PMT SN377, LVT 694. These Potteries CVD6s proved to be the last of a long line of second-hand Daimlers purchased by AICASA *(M. Dryhurst)*.

54

Above Sheffield United Tours 186 and 190, LWE 886/890 were exported to the Canary Islands in 1959 entering service in the APJG fleet on the island of Gran Canaria. Both were 1950 AEC Regal IIIs of the crash gearbox, 7.7-litre engined 6821A model with fully fronted Windover coachwork. In APJG ownership the Regals assumed a very different lifestyle, their bodies being converted to B29D layout for stage operation, GC-14561, formerly Sheffield United 190 being seen thus employed in Las Palmas in 1961. In addition to these Regal IIIs, three Windover-bodied Regal IVs from the same source could also be found running in Gran Canaria in the 1960s with other operators, NWB 204, OWB 211 and OWB 215 being the vehicles concerned *(M. Dryhurst)*.

Below Six former Sheffield United Tours AEC Regal 0662s of the 1948 JWE-registered batch went east to Yugoslavia in 1955. One of them, re-registered C.5316 is seen here in that year in service in Belgrade with its Windover body suitably converted for operation on the right. So far it has not been possible to obtain the exact identity of this vehicle although it would be one of the series SUT 141, 2, 3, 7, 50 or 52 registered JWE 641, etc *(J.C. Gillham)*.

Left Although British bus operators faced severe difficulties following the war, their problems were relatively minor when compared with those of bus operators in countries which had been under German occupation. In Holland, for example, in 1945 transport was urgently required in the coal mining area of Limburg in the south of the country and so a mixture of elderly single- and double-deckers was rapidly acquired by the Limburgsche Tramweg Maatschappij (LTM) and placed in service. This very interesting photograph depicts LTM 402, P.36164 one of five ex-East Yorkshire Motor Services lowbridge all Leyland TD1s of 1930 in the fleet, this particular vehicle originally being East Yorkshire 154, KH 9985 *(J. Voerman)*.

Left In August 1959 this former Northern General AEC Regent II with Northern Coachbuilders body was operating in Split, Yugoslavia. It is one of about six of the type which were exported to the country in 1957 following a period of ten or eleven years of operation with Northern. It will be noted that the rear entrance, and presumably the stairs, too, have been transposed to suit driving on the right. As with so many exported vehicles, the precise identity of H.11691 is unknown, although it can be stated that it is one of the batch registered ACN 167-176, new in 1946 *(D.W.K. Jones)*.

Right After rebuilding with offside entrances, a number of former Southdown Leyland Tigers were exported by Haulgo, the Havant dealer, around 1960, possibly to North Africa. This unregistered example seen shortly after refurbishing and prior to export is one of the Duple-bodied HUF registered batch of PS1s delivered with half cab rear entrance bodies in 1947-9 and then later rebuilt with Beadle full fronts and front entrances as a modernisation exercise *(R.H.G. Simpson)*.

Right Belgian operators faced severe transport difficulties following the retreat of the Wermacht in 1945 with second-hand vehicles being acquired from United Kingdom operators for public service. This Leyland Tiger, photographed at Ostend Railway Station shortly before withdrawal in 1957, was operated for many years on a Belgian Railways' contract between Ostend and Oudenberg by a now ceased operator, Deschepper Tousseyn, of the latter town. The UK identity of 3915.P, which earlier was registered 438986, is not known although the author suspects that it may well be one of the many Eastern Coachworks bodied TS8s once operated by Western Welsh *(D.W.K. Jones)*.

Right The chassis of Ribble 933, FCK 433, a 1953 Leyland Royal Tiger PSU1/16 originally with a Burlingham Seagull body, forms the basis of this Maltese coach owned by Zarb of Gzira. The attractive 36-seat body was built in 1975 by Frank Aquilina of Paola, one of a number of highly accomplished coach-builders on the island *(M. Fenton)*.

Above The China Motor Bus Company of Hong Kong acquired just over 100 former Southdown Leyland PD3s with fully fronted Northern Counties bodies, PD10, AH 4185 being one of the first arrivals in August 1972. Originally this bus was Southdown 819, TCD 819, one of the earliest PD3s bought by the company, in 1958 *(D. Withers).*

Below Many operators in New South Wales, Australia, acquired second-hand Leyland Atlanteans from Britain in the 1970s for school contract work, the high seating capacity and low purchase price of these buses making them a very attractive proposition. Joyces' Bus Company of Urunga purchased three Atlanteans in 1976, two of which were immediately sold to other operators with the third, MO·4210, retained for use by Joyces' themselves. This highbridge, Metro-Cammell-bodied PDR1/1 was new in 1961 to the then independent Scout fleet as PRN 144, becoming S4 when Ribble assumed control later in the same year. When the Scout fleet was fully absorbed by Ribble in 1968 it became Ribble 1972 *(B.A. Tilley).*

A SOUTH AFRICAN INTERLUDE

In view of the country's historical links with Britain, it is not surprising that South African operators should have purchased buses which would have been very much at home in many a United Kingdom fleet.

City of Pretoria Transport Department (Stedelike Vervoer Pretoria) 305, TP 107-904, is one of a small batch of PDR1/1 Leyland Atlanteans with MCW style Busaf bodywork which entered service in 1961 *(D.A. Lewis)*

Left Despite its claim to be a Leyland, City of Pretoria 369, TP 75158 is in reality a Daimler Road-liner, one of a batch of 27 purchased by this South African municipality in 1972. These Road-liners, which were the last of this unhappy model to be built, were noteworthy in being the only production examples powered by the 12.1L British Leyland V8 engine. Logically they received the designation SRL8. The simple yet attractive bodywork on the ilustrated example was built by Transvaal Motor Body Builders, although two other South African companies—Springfield Body Builders and Bus Bodies (South Africa)—each bodied buses from this batch *(D.A. Lewis)*.

Left Many South African operators took Daimler CV series chassis in the post-war years but only City Tramways of Cape Town had the special three-axle CVG6/6DD type as exemplified by CA-59109. A total of 20 were delivered in 1949 all of which had 64-seat Weymann bodywork and, additionally, the huge exposed radiator which was later to become associated with the CD650 model *(G. Shields)*.

Left City Tramways, Cape Town MO876, CA-16445, is one of a number of Leyland Titan OPD2/9s purchased in the mid-1950s by this operator which had bodies built by Bus Bodies (South Africa) of Port Elizabeth, a builder usually referred to as Busaf *(D.A. Lewis)*.

Above East London No 17, CE-12237, which was in its twentieth year of service when photographed in March 1969, is one of a batch of ten Weymann-bodied Daimler CVG5 buses bought by this South African municipality in 1949 *(G. Shields)*.

Below The exposed radiator Leyland Tiger PS apart from the odd exception ceased to be sold in the United Kingdom from the early 1950s. This was not, however, the case elsewhere for the largest model in the range, the 35 ft long PS4, continued in production until as late as 1968. Many were exported to South African customers, the illustration depicting 274, CB-51041, an OPS4/5 with Busaf bodywork in the Bay Passenger Transport fleet, a company formed in 1953 to serve the black townships around Port Elizabeth in Cape Province *(G. Shields)*.

Above Johannesburg Municipal Transport 662 is one of a batch of 50 three-axle BUT 9642Ts with Park Royal style Bus Bodies bodywork. When delivered in 1958 these fine vehicles had two-door bodywork but several were subsequently rebuilt as front entrance only, for one-man operation *(D.A. Lewis)*.

Below Numerically Johannesburg's final trolleybuses were Sunbeam S7As with 85-seat Bus Bodies two-door bodywork, the batch of 20, Nos 694-713, entering service in 1958 *(D.A. Lewis)*.

IMAGES OF IBERIA

Where else in 1980 could one find Sentinel, Maudslay and Atkinson buses still in use other than in Portugal? Added to these are half cab double-deckers and a variety of other models straight out of the pages of history. A similar choice used to exist in Spain, too, before the march of progress in the shape of the Pegaso sent many rareties to the scrapyard.

After a number of attempts at motor-bus operation in Lisbon had failed, regular operation finally became a reality in 1946 when a batch of six Weymann B28D-bodied AEC *Regents* entered service with the Companhia Carris de Ferro de Lisboa (CCFL). To be strictly correct these buses re-entered service as they had been used for a short time during 1940 in conjunction with the Portuguese World Exhibition at Belém before being placed in store for the duration of World War 2. To augment the Regents a real mish-mash of vehicles was delivered to CCFL in the early post-war period, operators both at home and overseas being grateful for any chassis, whatever the make, at this time. Among the most interesting of all deliveries were two all-Leyland PD1s of 1947 which, apart from the right-hand entrance, were the standard home market 56-seat bus. II-13-09 (CCFL 201) was nearing the end of its passenger-carrying career when photographed during 1973 at the Amoreiras depot, although still in obviously good order *(M. Fenton)*.

Left 1948 saw CCFL taking delivery of small numbers of Leyland OPS1, Albion Valkyrie CX13 and Maudslay Marathon III chassis, all of which were right-hand drive. The Maudslays received new ckd Weymann B32D bodies in 1952 to replace the original inferior local bodywork, although right-hand drive was retained. In 1964 the batch of five vehicles was withdrawn and one bus, CCFL 142 (GC-13-11), sold to a small plastics company in the western suburbs of Lisbon. Astonishingly this veteran remained in daily use as staff transport until June 1980 when a combination of rain and Lisbon's stone setts provided it with the perfect opportunity to demolish the rear end of a new CCFL Volvo B59. The writer was, however, assured by the owners that the Marathon would be repaired and returned to service as damage was not too severe. One of the Albions, likewise rebodied, lasted well, surviving until at least 1971 as a staff bus with a different company but also in the Lisbon area *(M. Fenton)*.

Centre left As supplies of new buses became more readily available, CCFL began to standardise on AECs with just over 100 Regal III 0963 and 9613E models being received in the late 1940s. The body contract for these was split between Saunders and Weymann, the former having a slightly greater share of the business. The Saunders-bodied examples were almost all rebodied in the latter half of the 1960s as double-deckers echoing British practice of a few years earlier, but nearly all the Weymanns continued as single-deckers after being rebuilt and extended at the rear. CCFL 137, IL-14-31 seen here in the Rua Alexandre Herculano, is one of the 1969 Weymann-CCFL rebuilds which differed from those rebuilt in the previous year in having the exit in a more forward position immediately behind the front bulkhead *(M. Fenton)*.

Left Four of CCFL's Saunders-bodied AEC Regal IIIs were rebodied with Weymann H30/26R bodywork after a very short period of service, No 247, GD-14-99 being so treated in 1954. In rebodied form they were indistinguishable from Lisbon's Regent IIIs, over 100 of which entered service between 1950 and 1957 *(M. Fenton)*.

Right Following the Portuguese revolution of April 1974, which saw a left-wing government take power, the larger private bus companies were nationalised, an action which brought in its wake modernisation of these fleets and the consequent demise of a number of rarities. One such fleet was that of Arboricultora Lda, based at Caneças, a suburb of Lisbon some 10 km to the north west of the city. At the time of nationalisation the company had approximately 80 buses including three Daimler Freelines which had been rebodied by UTIC (União de Transportadores para Importacao e Comércio), one of this trio being GD-56-35, a 1957 D650HS rebodied in 1971. Following nationalisation this vehicle became 6094 in the Rodoviaria Nacional (RN) but retained Arboricultora colours of chrome yellow and pink until withdrawn in 1976 *(M. Fenton)*.

Centre right Dutfield's of Godalming, Surrey, were just one of many coachbuilders in production during the early post-war boom period, bodies being constructed for a variety of chassis although Tilling-Stevens and Vulcans figured largely in the company's order books. Of great interest were two left-hand drive Perkins-engined Vulcan 6PF chassis with Dutfield bodywork exported to Portugal where they entered service in 1949 with Sintra-Atlântico, a small bus and tram operator based on Sintra, a historic town 30 km north-west of Lisbon. GG-16-05 is one of the pair photographed in 1965 at Praia das Macãs. Both were withdrawn during the early 1970s outlasting Dutfield-bodied Vulcans in the United Kingdom by a considerable margin! *(A.R. Phillips)*.

Right AEC Regent Vs were taken into CCFL ownership from 1958 when a batch with elegant Weymann bodywork, having similarities of design to the Regent IIIs, was delivered. Another consignment of Weymann-bodied Mk Vs followed in 1960 along with some outwardly similar UTIC-bodied examples. 1961-2, however, saw CCFL themselves body several Regent Vs again to the same Weymann style, one of the 1962 delivery CCFL 610, IA-30-16 being illustrated at the Praça do Comércio *(M. Fenton)*.

Above Isidoro Duarte of Povoa da Galega continues to this day to operate interesting vehicles although IC-15-36 shown here was withdrawn around 1976. It was the only Crossley ever to run in Portugal, an SD42/2 of 1949 rebodied in the 1960s by UTIC, a Leyland engine being fitted at about the same time. The SD42/2 was an 18 ft wheelbase export model, the vast majority of which were sold to the Netherlands' Railways who took over 400 units *(M. Fenton)*.

Below This Sentinel SLC6 of Isidoro Duarte was one of only two examples of the make to come to Portugal. This rare view shows BL-18-52 in original condition with what is believed to be Pereira & Fausto Crespo bodywork. During the 1960s it was rebodied by UTIC and a Leyland engine and pneumocyclic gearbox installed; it continued in this much rebuilt form until at least 1979 when the author noted it in service near Lisbon. The other Sentinel which operated for a number of operators in central Portugal was also rebodied by UTIC but unlike the Duarte vehicle was withdrawn some years ago and last seen in derelict condition at the RN garage, Sernache *(A. G. Johnson)*.

Right A mixed bag of buses could be found in pre-nationalisation days in the Bucelense fleet at Bucelas and Tojal. A visit in 1973 revealed a right-hand drive Daimler CVD6, two Leyland Tiger PS3s, a Maudslay Marathon III, a Leyland Royal Tiger LOPSU1 and, illustrated, a right-hand drive Poden PVSC6 of 1949. Yes, a *Poden*. Really, of course, it *is* a Foden but unfortunately the name has a rather naughty meaning in Portuguese and was thus changed to Poden so as not to cause offence. All Portuguese Fodens were similarly labelled. Inevitably the body is yet another UTIC product dating from the early 1960s. Rebodying of chassis is considered the norm in Portugal hence the large number of chassis which are so treated each year *(M. Fenton)*.

Below right To the Portuguese the town of Coimbra is best known for its university, one of the oldest in Europe although students of transport would almost certainly find the buses, trams and trolleys of the SMC (Serviços Municipalizados de Coimbra) of greater interest. Coimbra's trolleybus system, the first in Portugal, commenced in 1947 using two Swiss-built Saurers which proved to be the only non-British trolleybuses purchased new by SMC. No 24 shown here was one of six Park Royal B40D-bodied Sunbeam MF2B chassis with BTH equipment delivered in 1950, a sister vehicle, 23 being exhibited at that year's Commercial Motor Show. During the latter half of the 1970s the Park Royal bodies on these vehicles were scrapped and smart new Salvador Caetano bodies fitted. Three Park Royal-bodied BUT LETB/1s delivered in 1954 were similarly treated at the same time. Coimbra additionally has BUT LETB/1s with UTIC bodies and Sunbeam MF2Ns, the last built, plus rebodied Henschels, purchased from Braga when that system closed down in 1980 *(M. Fenton)*.

Left Many amazing vehicles may be found in the hills of central Portugal, this odd looking normal control machine being none other than a 1948 Bedford OB rebodied after about 20 years of service by UTIC! Portuguese normal control chassis often received new bonnets in place of the manufacturer's standard fitment, sometimes as a result of accident damage or more usually in the way of a modernisation exercise as in the case of AL-13-34. The OB, photographed in Celorico da Beira, is owned by Viúva Carneiro & Filhos (widow Carneiro & sons) whose fleet has its headquarters in the small town of Meda *(M. Fenton)*.

Below This Guy Otter/UTIC of 1958 still in original condition was photographed in the village of Satão in 1980. It is just one of a clutch of rarities owned by the União de Satão e Aguiar da Beira fleet whose buses may be found

scattered over a wide area to the north and east of Viseu. Some of these gems included, in 1980, a Maudslay Marathon III, a normal control Fordson ETF7, a brace of Albion Viking VK41Ls and a Ford R1114 believed to be the only one of its kind in Portugal. Operators such as this generally escaped compulsory nationalisation, their size being the critical factor *(M. Fenton)*.

Right The day in 1979 that five foreigners arrived in the remote Portuguese village of Sobral and proceded to photograph a bus will probably be spoken of for years to come! About half the population of the village observed with interest the unusual spectacle along with a goatherd, his flock of goats and a couple of emaciated dogs! Of course, this was no ordinary bus being one of a dozen or so Maudslay Regal III M9631Rs built in AEC's badge engineering days in the early 1950s. Although the owner, Manuel Pacheco, was based in the town of Lamego, the Regal operated in Guarda over 100 km distant, Sobral being the village where it was outstationed. Alfredo Caetano of Vila Nova de Gaia, Porto, one of a number of coach-building Caetanos, built the body on ED-18-73 *(M. Fenton)*.

Right 1948 saw the inauguration of motor-bus services in Oporto when the STCP (Servico de Transportes Colectivos do Porto) placed a total of 30 right-hand drive Daimler CVD6s in service. The next motor-buses, delivered in 1952, were supplied by AEC being Regal III 9631E models bodied by the STCP themselves. PT-13-52 illustrates the type. Over the years the eight buses in this batch were subjected to various degrees of rebuilding with window lines and radiator grilles especially differing from vehicle to vehicle *(M. Fenton)*.

Left Oporto is a comparative newcomer to the ranks of trolleybus operators, the STCP commencing as late as 1959 with a fleet of 20 BUT LETB/1s with Park Royal inspired two-door UTIC bodies. A second batch of basically similar BUTs followed in 1963, although these buses had three-door bodywork and consequently a lower seating capacity, one of these being illustrated nearing the Bolhão terminus in the centre of Oporto. At the time of writing, although Oporto buses, trolleys and trams are all operated by the same undertaking, no fewer than four different liveries may be seen; trams are light brown and cream, trolleybuses cherry red, cream and grey and motor-buses either the current orange and cream or earlier turquoise and ivory! *(M. Fenton).*

Left Several Portuguese independents have built their own bodywork, sometimes utilising framing supplied by UTIC. PO-15-14 displays the skills of the bodybuilding shops of the União de Transportes dos Carvalhos, a smart medium-sized Oporto area operator based at Perozinho. Under the Carvalhos body is an Atkinson LPL746 chassis of 1955, the only one in this fleet and indeed a make never common throughout the rest of Portugal *(M. Fenton).*

Left IA-61-22 is one of ten Leyland Atlanteans bodied by the local builder, Salvador Caetano of Vila Nova de Gaia, for the STCP in 1962. It will be noted that upper and lower deck windows are of unequal depth on this bus, a feature reminiscent of MCW bodies of the period. This is not really surprising as Metro-Cammell assisted Caetano in building the bodies, indeed the prototype had MCW framing. Later STCP Atlanteans included, in 1963, some with Dalfa bodies and then in 1966 another batch with Caetano bodies, although at 10 m these were longer than the first batch *(M. Fenton).*

Above Home-made bodywork is carried by this early Guy Arab LHUF of Auto Viacão Feirense Lda of Lourosa. Since this shot of BG-19-03 was taken the body has been replaced by a standard UTIC product *(M. Fenton)*.

Below This 1956 Daimler Freeline D650HS/Alfredo Caetano was in absolutely original condition when seen in Oporto in 1977 still with its Daimler engine and preselective gearbox. It is one of 27 examples of the model supplied to various Portuguese operators between 1955 and 1960, the owner of EG-24-16 for its entire working life being Auto Viacão Landim of Felgueiras. As with many Portuguese buses the livery is worthy of note being an unusual combination of pale pink, light grey and white! *(M. Fenton)*.

Above The first Leyland Royal Tiger Worldmasters for the Spanish capital, Madrid, were exactly 100 LERT1s of 1957 with B24T standee style MCW bodies, M·188576 being Empresa Municipal de Transportes 581. Further Worldmasters for this operator followed in 1959 and 1960 with some being later rebodied by private owners for further operation *(G. Elliott).*

Left No 56, SS·12625 of the San Sebastián municipal fleet, Tranvía de San Sebastián, is one of eight right-hand drive Leyland Tiger OPS1s of 1948 which were rebodied about 1960 by the Spanish builder Irizar *(G. Elliott).*

Left The six-wheeled single-door trolleybus being overtaken by an ex-London Q1 was one of 25 BUT 9641Ts bought new by Tranvía de San Sebastián. These vehicles would appear to have been highly successful in one respect; that of wearing out bodywork, for No 27, which is typical of the batch, is carrying its *third* body in less than 15 years, this time by Irizar! The Q1 is also, coincidentally, one of a batch of 25; San Sebastián 71-95 acquired in 1961/2 *(A.R. Phillips).*

Above Valencia's early post-war bus fleet contained a small batch of eight or nine handsome half cab, half canopy OPS1 Leyland Tigers which had locally constructed dual-door bodywork. This shot shows Valenciana de Autobuses SA 116, V·22505 working on the Estación Norte — Grao route in 1952 *(N.N. Forbes)*.

Right Some very strange double-deckers are known to have operated around Bilbao in the Basque Province of northern Spain. Transportes Urbanos del Gran Bilbao SA (TUGB) 230 BI·33388, consists of an underfloor-engined Leyland Royal Tiger Worldmaster chassis with 72-seat Logrona bodywork of exceedingly restricted upper deck headroom *(G. Elliott)*.

Right This fine double-deck sightseeing coach, GE·60509, which entered service in 1966 consists of a right-hand drive Leyland Atlantean PDR1/1 chassis with 60-seat central entrance bodywork by Ayats of Arbucias. It was built for the company Pullmantur SA and at first worked in Madrid, although by the time this shot was taken in 1971 it had moved to Barcelona, a Daimler Roadliner with *double-deck* Irizar coachwork having taken its place in the Spanish capital *(B.A. Tilley)*.

Above Altogether Tranvías de Barcelona bought 70 left-hand drive, preselective AEC Regent IIIs between 1948 and 1953, with 492, B·85511, being representative of the final batch of 20. Rear entrance 61-seat bodywork by Materiales & Construcciones SA of Barcelona (Macosa) was fitted to these buses, built to the same design that the company had used when bodying the first Regents in 1948. The balance of 45 chassis received central entrance bodywork by Carde & Escoriaza of Zaragoza. Many of the Regents were subsequently rebodied as single-deckers by Seida of Bilbao *(J.H. Price)*.

Left This right-hand drive AEC Regal III, M·115727, with fully fronted Ramos coachwork was operating for the company SOLVYT (Sociedad de Viajes y Transportes Lda) when photographed in Valencia during October 1966 *(G. Elliott)*.

Above Upon being declared redundant in London a total of 125 Q1 class BUT 9641T trolleybuses was exported to Spanish operators during the early 1960s. Three of the five vehicles sold for service in Pontevedra, with Tranvía Electrico de Pontevedra, unusually kept their open rear platforms, albeit transposed to the right-hand side, and additionally remained as 70-seaters. Livery was pale blue and cream and, as may be seen from the illustration of 103, maintenance was of a high standard. Originally this vehicle was London Transport 1811, HYM 811 *(J.G.S. Smith).*

Right The forward control Leyland Comet 90, the ECP02 model, was popular for a time with some Spanish operators, this right-hand drive example in the fleet of Empresa el Oriete, C·8619, being typical of those placed in service during the 1950s *(G. Elliott).*

Left The year 1960 saw 15 of Rotherham Corporation's distinctive Daimler CTC6 trolleybuses exported for further use in Spain. Interestingly, although their new owner, Tranvías de Zaragoza, was based in the province of Aragon in northern Spain, these buses were bought for operation in Cádiz which is in the south-west of the country. In their new home they received fleet numbers 11-25 and ran with their original East Lancashire bodies rebuilt to a rear entrance/front exit layout, 15 wooden seats being provided for those hardy Spaniards who wished to avail themselves of this dubious privilege. A further pair of identical vehicles was purchased by the same company in 1961 and similarly rebuilt, but this time for use in Tolosa in the Basque region *(D. Trevor Rowe).*

Since the closure of the border with Spain in 1967, bus services in Gibraltar have declined and coach tours completely ceased. In pre-1967 days many of the buses operating in Gibraltar were worthy of attention, some being bought new and others at second-hand. This picture contrasts sharply with the present situation where the bus population consists mainly of small-capacity vehicles with Ford Transits and Commer minibuses forming the bulk.

Below G·6055 is one of five left-hand drive Bedford OB chassis with Duple bodies delivered to Gibraltar Motorways in 1946. By the time this photograph was taken in October 1961 it had acquired a rear axle reminiscent of those fitted to military vehicles with what appear to be 10.50-16 tyres on single rear wheels. Although this bus was scrapped several years ago, the company continues to operate, albeit on a small scale, with just one route from the town to Sandy Bay *(M. Dryhurst).*

Above The Gibraltarian operator Whitelock Tours, which ceased some years ago, was considerably smaller than Gibraltar Motorways but made up for this by having a fascinating fleet of mainly second-hand stock. Only one route was worked by the company, route 6 to Rosia, G·12142, a 1938 Bedford WTB/Duple, once Southern Vectis 207, CDL 729, being shown working this service. Like a number of other buses on 'the Rock' this bus has a peculiar over bodied appearance due to the use of a rear axle having single wheels *(M. Dryhurst)*.

Below Few buses were bought new by Whitelock Tours but G·7038 must be included in this number. It is one of a pair of left-hand drive Morris Commercials with 27-seat Wadham bodies. Although the precise chassis type is not known it would seem likely that the FV12/5 model was used, this being basically a goods chassis on sale in the period 1949-53 *(M. Dryhurst)*.

Above G·11011 is another of Whitelock Tours' second-hand acquisitions in the shape of an ex-Red & White pre-war Albion Valiant. In Gibraltar, where driving is on the right, the Duple B35C body was slightly modified so as to use the offside emergency exit as the normal means of entry. So far it has not been possible to identify the exact vehicle concerned and the author would be pleased to hear from any reader who is able to resolve this query *(M. Dryhurst)*.

Below Scottish Aviation of Prestwick built the body on this Albion Victor FT39 which is another of Whitelock Tours' as yet unidentified ex-United Kingdom second-hand bargains. The Victor FT built in the late 1940s and the 1950s was popular with operators both at home and overseas. It was usually powered by Albion's own four-cylinder diesel engine, although a six-cylinder petrol-engined chassis, the FT3AB, was also offered *(M. Dryhurst)*.

THE BENELUX COUNTRIES

In terms of British-made buses the Benelux countries, Belgium, the Netherlands and Luxembourg, constitute an area of abundance surrounded by the desert of France and Germany.

Trolleybuses first appeared in the Netherlands during 1927 when the town of Groningen introduced a limited service using two 24-seat, front entrance Daimlers. The system expanded, reaching its peak in 1960, but then rapidly declined closing completely in 1965. During the 1930s Groningen's trolleybus network had been studied by Arnhem Tramways (Gemeente Tram Arnhem) who were contemplating the introduction of this mode of transport to augment their tramway system. World War 2, however, put an end to such plans but by a roundabout way also ensured that the trolleybus would ultimately be introduced, for much of the tram track was damaged and the depot and rolling stock destroyed during the Battle of Arnhem. Following the Liberation in 1945, Arnhem's tramway was officially abandoned and trolleybuses eventually introduced in September 1949. The first vehicles of the undertaking, now retitled Gemeente Vervoerbedrijf Arnhem, were 16 English Electric-equipped BUT 9721Ts with Verheul bodies. In the following years extensions were made to the system and further Verheul-bodied BUTs appeared in 1950, 1955 and 1956, 142 (XB-08-25) being one of the final batch all of which are now withdrawn. Nine years passed before the next batch of trolleys appeared in Arnhem, these being based on the Leyland-Verheul motor-bus of the period, and these continue to serve the town along with later DAFs *(I. Charlton)*.

Above Because of a shortage of suitable purpose-built PSV chassis, demobilised military trucks suitably converted or completely rebodied formed the basis of many Dutch passenger vehicles in the years following the end of the war. The Bedford OWL 5-tonner was an especially popular choice, sometimes converted to forward control. Other chassis used included Austins; this 1943 K2 type 2-tonner, K.17545, received a 20-seat Jongerius bus body in 1948 for NV Stoomtram of Walcheren *(J. Voerman)*.

Above left Post-war Holland was an especially lucrative market for Crossley who sold a total of 1,175 chassis to the Netherlands Railways companies between 1947 and 1949. Three models were involved; the PT42/1 normal control passenger tractor for use with semi-trailer, the SD42/1 'Long Dutch' and SD42/2 'Short Dutch' with respectively 250, 500 and 425 vehicles being supplied. With the exception of a relatively small number of SD42/2s which had Crossley-built bodies, bodywork was built by a variety of Dutch firms. NV Nederlandsche Buurtspoorweg Maatschappij

(NBM) of Zeist 2121 was an SD42/2 bodied in 1949 by Schelde under licence from Verheul. It remained in service until 1961 receiving the registration NB-64-58 in the early 1950s in place of provincial (Utrecht) registration L-55171 *(J. Voerman).*

Bottom left The 25 10.9 m Leyland Nationals delivered to the Netherlands Railways in 1975 were split between four subsidiary companies with Nord-Zuid Hollandse (NZH) taking seven and the remaining companies—Centraal Nederland (CN), Westnederland (WN) and Zuid-Ooster (ZO)—six each. After two years of service, following complaints from drivers about reflections of interior lights at night, the Nationals' windscreens were replaced by more or less standard lantern type Dutch screens. NZH 3106, 02-37-HB, is seen here in the centre of Haarlem in April 1977 shortly after rebuilding *(M. Fenton).*

Above right Two prototype Park Royal-bodied AEC Regal IVs were built in 1949, one with right-hand drive and one with left-hand drive, the latter example being built to the larger dimensions permissible in Europe at that time with a 17 ft 6 in wheelbase suitable for bodywork up to 10 m. Several Dutch operators, including the Hague Tramways (HTM) and the Geldersche Tramwegen (GTW), had it on extended and obviously successful trial for both ordered Regal IVs in quantity. Under the old provincial registration system used in Holland at that time, vehicles were re-registered on being sold or transferred, the number staying with the operator for re-use. This shot shows the Regal with GTW when it had Gelderland registration M-31096. By the mid-1950s it had returned to the United Kingdom for non-PSV use *(J. Voerman).*

Centre right RB-72-80 is one of a batch of 38 Verheul-bodied 9832E AEC Regal IVs delivered in 1956 to the Hague Tramways (Haagsche Tramweg Maatschappij). The Regal IV was especially popular in the Dutch capital, HTM taking a grand total of 118 over the years 1952 to 1959 *(W. Vink).*

Right A total of six Guy Victory chassis received bodies by Domburg of Montfoort between 1959 and 1966 all of them going to the nearby company Verenigde Auto-busdiensten Gouda–Utrecht (VAGU) of Oudewater. The final example, VAGU 52, AB-27-61 was noteworthy in being the only one to have a dual door body, the seating capacity being 48 with space for a further 32 standees *(M. Fenton).*

Above The four AEC Monocoaches supplied to the Netherlands Railways in the mid-1950s seem to have led quite sheltered lives with little ever appearing in print about them. Three different Dutch coachbuilders supplied bodies on Monocoach 'chassis' that on NACO of Alkmaar 6200 (PN-45-08) being a den Oudsten product of 1957. Both this bus and GADO of Groningen 6201 were of a special short wheelbase model seating 39 passengers. The remaining two Monocoaches were of standard dimensions bodied by Verheul (B45D) and Hainje (DP49F) in 1955 and 1956 respectively. All four had chassis numbers in the experimental U series *(W. Vink)*.

Below The reason why this left-hand drive Harrington C28D-bodied Dennis Lancet should have gone to the Netherlands is not clear, however, the most plausible explanation is that it was sent over as a demonstrator. The chassis, No 170563 dating from 1934, is one of the original Mark I Lancets built between 1932 and 1936, although by the time this photograph was taken in 1947 it had acquired a rather inadequate looking replacement front axle as well as a Volvo petrol engine. As shown HZ 38211 was operating for WSM of Loosduinen but its original Dutch owner was Leguit of Soesterberg, Utrecht, with whom it was registered L-6848 *(J. Voerman)*.

Right Early post-war coaching in the Netherlands followed a very similar path to that of Britain with a great demand for travel producing a boom period during which many small coachbuilders flourished and then faded away, some especially flamboyant styles being devised during this time. One of the survivors was van Rooyen who bodied this Austin CXD in 1951 for Labeto Tours of Amsterdam. The provincial registration (GZ-98883) of this coach was later replaced by national registration NB-54-77 *(Van Rooyen)*.

Right One of the most successful of all exported British chassis is the ubiquitous Bedford SB with sales running into several thousand. The model was quite popular for a time in Holland, TB-70-70 being one of a number of basically similar SBs bodied by the Belgian coachbuilder Van Hool for a Dutch dealer. This particular vehicle, which dates from 1960, has the SB1 chassis and was used until 1978 by Thijssen of Geulle *(I. Charlton)*.

Below right The smart two-tone blue liveried fleet of Henri Nefkens of Amersfoort took many Leylands including Dutch-built examples such as the Leyland Holland Coach, which used Tiger Cub units and the Leyland-Verheul LV45 using Albion Viking parts. Nefkens No 5 is, however, an English-built Leyland, a Tiger Cub LOPSUC1/1 with Verheul C37F coachwork. Like most Dutch PSVs of the 1950s and 1960s, the letter B prefixed by another letter is used in its registration, TB-80-57 being one of the 1960 series which ran from TB-61-17 through to UB-16-33 *(M. Fenton)*.

Left Limburg Province in the extreme south of Holland has had some interesting operators of British-built buses and coaches within its bounds. The now ceased company White Cars of Heerlen retained until the end a fleet of elderly raised deck coaches which included Bussings, not of interest as far as this volume is concerned, and Leylands; a Royal Tiger Cub/Kusters of 1960 and a Royal Tiger of 1953 rebodied by Smit of Joure in the mid-1960s. The shot of Royal Tiger NB-80-51 was taken in London, near Victoria Station in the summer of 1975 whilst it was on a tour of Britain! The exact type and chassis number of this fine vehicle are not known but it may be safely assumed that the standard 17 ft 6 in wheelbase LOPSU1/2 chassis would have been used *(M. Fenton)*.

Left For a while the Leyland Leopard was popular with Dutch operators, this Roset-bodied PSU3/1L (XB-72-05) being new in 1964 to a company from Holten in Overijssel province named Overijsselsche Autobus Diensten BV, or OAD for short *M. Fenton)*.

Left The forward control (18 ft 2 in) wheelbase Guy Warrior was introduced in 1956 ostensibly as a replacement for the Vixen even though it was longer and heavier than its predecessor. Apart from Plaxton-bodied JBV 234, the Warrior was sold exclusively on the export market with several joining the fleet of Snel of Pernis. Many of Snel's vehicles were later purchased by another Dutch operator Betuwe Express of Herveld, including Bova-bodied ZB-51-97 which was new in 1965 *(M. Fenton)*.

Right With the exception of one small forward control vehicle, all the DAFs bodied by Plaxton for the Dutch market have been 11 m, rear-engined SB series chassis. At the time of writing more than 70 are in service. Apart from a very small number of Viewmasters, Supreme coachwork was specified for those built between 1976 and 1978, the Supreme IV then making its appearance in 1979. Oostenrijk of Diemen were the owners of 40-TB-85, a 1980 Supreme IV bodied SB2005 photographed in April 1981 at Keukenhof, a place famous for its bulb fields some 15 km south of Haarlem *(M. Fenton)*.

Right Five different companies in Luxembourg still had British-made stock in the late 1970s with AEC being the dominant make and the Regal VI the most popular model. The well kept Demy Cars fleet of J. Schandeler, Keispelt, with its York Pullman-like livery had six Regal VIs, 87074 consisting of a 12 m mono-control U2LA chassis and 55-seat Van Hool bodywork, new in 1964 *(M. Fenton)*.

Right This 1958 AEC Regal IV 9834S of Josy Clement, Bourglinster, was rebodied in 1972 by Comes, a Luxembourg bodybuilder, producing what must be a unique combination of chassis and body. This interesting individual was cornered in the village of Godbrange after working a service from Luxembourg City. A marginally older Jonckheere-bodied MU3LA Reliance was still used by the company in 1980 *(M. Fenton)*.

Left The Belgian coachbuilder Van Hool is a comparative newcomer to the industry being founded in the immediate post-war period by Mr Bernard Van Hool in the village of Koningshooikt near Lier. A very wide range of British-made chassis was bodied right from the start for Belgian customers including AEC, Austin, Bedford, Commer, Guy, Leyland and Maudslay. But what is the make shown you may well ask, studying the elaborate but unfamiliar lines of this vehicle's wings and bonnet? Answer, the voluminous metalwork hides none other than a humble Bedford OB! Such modifications to normal control passenger chassis were common in Belgium at this time with the OB, for example, being considered a little dated in appearance when something more ostentatious was required *(Van Hool)*.

Left The Guy Victory, introduced in 1958, once featured prominently in several Belgian fleets but few survived into the 1980s. One exception was BBK-987, a 1962 Leyland 0.680-engined example with Jonckheere 50-seat coackwork, which was still in regular use in 1981 as a school bus with J. Van Roey of Balen *(M. Fenton)*.

Below In addition to the well-known coachbuilding concern Van Hool, the town of Lier, near Antwerp, until a few years ago boasted another company which built bus and coach bodies; Stoelen. This old-established firm which started in the 1920s traded for many years as Bostovo, the name being a contraction of the original title Bogaerts, Stoelen & Van Ouystel. This Bedford VAL14 of 1964, which displays typical Stoelen bodywork of the period, is one of two in the interesting

L. Gevers van Hove 'De Blauwvoet' fleet of Balen in north-eastern Belgium. By the time this photograph was taken in early 1981, 327.P.7 was being powered by a DAF engine in place of its third worn out Leyland 0.400 *(M. Fenton).*

Right This impressive Guy Arab was supplied to an unknown operator in eastern Belgium in the late 1940s for use on a Belgian Railways contract between Liège and Vise. The Arab was popular in post-war Belgium with Van Hool bodying several of the 30 Arab IIs exported in 1945-6 as well as many more Arab IIIs, including this example *(Van Hool).*

Right The export only, AH690-engined AEC Regal VI was introduced in 1960 as a replacement for the Regal IV. Virtually all the Regal VIs sold in Belgium had the 19 ft 6 in wheelbase chassis suitable for 12 m bodywork of either bus or coach pattern. The small coaching side of the Van Hoorebeke fleet of Maldegem, which traded under the name 'Scotland Cars', put this Jonckheere-bodied U3LA in service in 1965, this version of the Regal VI having the ZF six-speed synchromesh gearbox *(M. Fenton).*

Below The AEC Regal IV was seldom sold for use in Britain after 1955, the lighter Reliance having taken its place. Overseas, though, Regal IVs continued to enter service, Lefever of Hooglede 5707.P being one of the last chassis built, a Monocontrol transmission 9835E of 1960 with Van Hool bodywork licensed to carry 80 passengers; 47 seated and 33 standing *(I. Charlton).*

Above This 1963 LCRT1/1 Leyland Worldmaster with Remi Desot of Gits bus bodywork is just one of an interesting British contingent in the fleet of Achiel Weyn & Zoon of Stekene. In addition to several more Worldmasters the company still had a number of Guys in 1981 including the last surviving Victory Trambus (front engined), two conventional Victorys—one second-hand from Holland—and a disused but intact Guy Arab III/Desot rebody *(M. Fenton)*.

Below Some parts of the Vicinal inter-urban tramway network remain along the coast and in the area of Charleroi, but most of this once extensive system is now operated by buses. Because two languages are used in Belgium the company is known as the Société Nationale des Chemins de Fer Vicinaux (SNCV) in the French-speaking region but the Nationale Maatschappij van Buurtspoorwegen (NMVB) in areas where Flemish is spoken. As an experiment, in 1979, the company took delivery of about 25 Leyland B21s bodied in Belgium by Jonckheere, one being shown here in service at Gent-Dampoort Station. The B21, apart from its front mounted radiator is really a National with a chassis, NMVB 5024, 0238.P, being type B21/1LS *(M. Fenton)*.